We need women like Sara Hage[...]
Adore—ushering us into the thr[...]
of the mundane and the maintenance. This is a book not to miss.
If you heed its encouragement, it will change your life.

— JESS CONNOLLY, AUTHOR, *YOU ARE THE GIRL FOR THE JOB*

Sara Hagerty's *Adore* is a beautiful invitation into the simple but
vital practice of drawing near to God. I love Sara's heart in continually pointing us to the real and lasting treasure of daily and even
minute-by-minute communion with God. This is where *real* life
happens as we allow His Word and His presence to meet us every
day, right where we are!

— CHRISTY NOCKELS, SINGER, SONGWRITER,
THE GLORIOUS IN THE MUNDANE PODCAST

The nearness and tenderness of God will be so real to you as you
read this book. Sara builds words in such a way it feels like God is
so near as you read them.

— JENNIE ALLEN, AUTHOR, *GET OUT OF YOUR HEAD*;
FOUNDER AND VISIONARY, IF:GATHERING

This book is a must-read, and one that I will go back to again and
again. As Sara shares her heart and stories, you feel so known and
understood and drawn to the Savior's feet to worship Him there, in
the midst of the storm and unknown and hard. This book was such
a timely tool for me to adore Him in the midst of my own heartache.

— ALYSSA BETHKE, AUTHOR, *LOVE THAT LASTS*

If you desire to have authentic intimacy with God and to understand how to cultivate peace and joy amid a demanding life, you
must read this book. Sara has written a book after my own heart's
values—finding God to be the source of light, beauty, truth, love
that we need every day.

— SALLY CLARKSON, AUTHOR, BLOGGER,
PODCASTER; SALLYCLARKSON.COM

The longing of Sara's heart is for God and His with-us presence. Her writing reveals glimpses into their holy relationship. Adoration is not a prayer technique but a response of our hearts to His unending invitation to be with Him every moment of every day. I pray this book becomes contagious! Nothing is more important.

—BARBARA RAINEY, CREATOR AND FOUNDER, EVER THINE HOME; COFOUNDER, FAMILY LIFE

Sara's words pour out like pure water, line after line, page after page, satiating a part of my heart I didn't know was suffering from thirst. Sara has an incredible way of drawing you into her story at the same time drawing you into a place where your heart tenderly acknowledges your need for God even in the smallest of moments throughout the day. Sara doesn't leave us there, as she also reveals the impact of His engaging presence as we look to Him and experience being known. *Adore* is more than a book, it is a pitcher of refreshment for the soul, healing balm for the heart, and a picture of God's enduring love for each and every one of us.

—JENNIFER SMITH, AUTHOR, THE UNVEILED WIFE AND MARRIAGE AFTER GOD

Sara Hagerty's voice of wisdom has long been one of my favorites, because of her consistency in pointing her readers toward the Word of God and the one who breathed it. In *Adore*, Sara beckons us to look for God where we might least expect Him, in the mundane middle of our days and our lives. Her words turn my gaze to Jesus, who calls me to know His heart for me in new ways. Sara takes God's Word and makes it real, using her own experiences to show us how to apply His truth to our lives and how to open wide the doors for a new kind of relationship with our Father. In a world full of easy escapes, *Adore* is a needed reminder to center our lives around Jesus. If you, like me, need a fresh vision of God's goodness in the midst of your ordinary, this book is for you. Come, feel His gaze on you! See how He loves you!

—KATIE DAVIS MAJORS, AUTHOR, KISSES FROM KATIE AND DARING TO HOPE

ADORE

Other Books by Sara Hagerty

*Every Bitter Thing Is Sweet: Tasting the
Goodness of God in All Things*

*Unseen: The Gift of Being Hidden in a
World That Loves to Be Noticed*

*The Gift of Limitations: Finding
Beauty in Your Boundaries*

ADORE

A SIMPLE PRACTICE FOR
EXPERIENCING GOD IN THE
MIDDLE MINUTES OF YOUR DAY

SARA HAGERTY

ZONDERVAN BOOKS

Adore
Copyright © 2020 by Sara Hagerty

Published in Grand Rapids, Michigan, by Zondervan. Zondervan is a registered trademark of The Zondervan Corporation, L.L.C., a wholly owned subsidiary of HarperCollins Christian Publishing, Inc.

Requests for information should be addressed to customercare@harpercollins.com.

Zondervan titles may be purchased in bulk for educational, business, fundraising, or sales promotional use. For information, please email SpecialMarkets@Zondervan.com.

ISBN 978-0-310-37002-4 (softcover)
ISBN 978-0-310-35703-2 (audio)

Library of Congress Cataloging-in-Publication Data
Names: Hagerty, Sara, 1977- author.
Title: Adore : a simple practice for experiencing God in the middle minutes of your day / Sara Hagerty.
Description: Grand Rapids : Zondervan, 2020. | Includes bibliographical references. | Summary: "For anyone who longs to experience God in the thick of life's demands, Sara Hagerty's Adore offers a simple, soul-nourishing practice for engaging with God in the middle minutes of your day"—Provided by publisher.
Identifiers: LCCN 2019049989 (print) | LCCN 2019049990 (ebook) | ISBN 9780310357001 (hardcover) | ISBN 9780310357025 (ebook)
Subjects: LCSH: Thought and thinking—Religious aspects—Christianity. | Awareness—Religious aspects—Christianity.
Classification: LCC BV4598.4 .H335 2020 (print) | LCC BV4598.4 (ebook) | DDC 248.2—dc23
LC record available at https://lccn.loc.gov/2019049989
LC ebook record available at https://lccn.loc.gov/2019049990

Published in association with Yates and Yates, www.yates2.com.

Cover design: James W. Hall IV
Cover photo: Good Vibration Images / Stocksy
Author photo: Cherish Andrea Photography
Interior design: Denise Froehlich

To my mom, Karen Welter.
You adored Him long before I understood it.
Thank you for this inheritance.

CONTENTS

ADORE:
THIRTY CHARACTERISTICS OF GOD
WITH WHICH TO ADORE HIM

FOREWORD

The contents of my purse were scattered across the sanc-
tuary floor, right where the people of our church receive
prayer after the Word is preached and sung on a Sunday
morning. I don't know why I did it, aside from the still, small
voice saying, "Pour out your purse here." I was alone. It was
a Tuesday morning.

An hour before this, I had been so angry. Angry as I
yanked clothes on my toddler. Angry as I prodded my other
two children into the minivan, running late to school again.
Angry as I recounted an argument my husband and I had the
night before. Angry at the person who cost me thirty precious
seconds as they looked at their phone when the light turned
green. More than all that, I was angry that I felt forgotten
and unseen by God.

*Why does everything have to be so hard for me? And why
am I so angry all the time?*

A friend called to catch up. The tremor in my voice told
on me. She prodded and I unloaded, but the weight refused
to lift. She suggested I read the beginning of 1 Samuel and
ask the Lord what He might have for me there. I pointed my
minivan toward the church, my mind set on finding relief

before Him. I know He isn't bound to a location. He can be found at the kitchen sink or in the car while I run errands. But my heart longed for a quiet place, and I happened to have time for it.

The pages of my Bible practically fell open to Hannah's prayer in 1 Samuel and her response to Eli, the high priest, when he accused her of being drunk at the doorpost of the temple of the Lord: "But Hannah answered, 'No, my lord, I am a woman troubled in spirit. I have drunk neither wine nor strong drink, but I have been pouring out my soul before the LORD'" (1 Sam. 1:15 ESV).

As I read those words, a dam broke. I let it all out—the disappointment and the anger, and the shame I felt as a result of those. My purse was a picture of the pouring out. I needed help seeing what it could look like to pour my heart out to the Lord—all the mess and all the gold. And I needed to see that the Lord would not reject me in that place. Instead, He would receive me so that I could do what my heart longed for: adore Him.

I didn't know that's what I was doing until I read Sara's words in this book. Through *Adore*, I have discovered a friend from afar who graciously invites me into her grit to behold and adore the God of the middle minutes. Her vulnerability helps me feel less alone in the struggle, and the grace she has found in communion with an unwavering God gives me hope for a life of adoration through the momentous and the mundane. Come, friend, and let us adore Him.

—LAUREN CHANDLER

My Grit Meets
His Beauty

Finding God Where We
Least Expect Him

For Christ plays in ten thousand places.

—GERARD MANLEY HOPKINS,
"AS KINGFISHERS CATCH FIRE"

Life is a total of minutes spent.

Attaching a bandaid to a child's wound.

Turning off the outdoor lights before bed.

Lugging the overloaded grocery bag to the kitchen counter.

Sending a text message.

Sifting through a stack of mail that's full of advertisements.

Powering off the computer.

Applying mascara.

At fifteen, when I gave "my whole life" to Jesus, I didn't consider that living the radical life for God would one day call forth minute-by-minute faithfulness of me. I gathered my fifteen years like a stack of files and foisted them on the one who'd been watchful, in exchange for a notepad we would fill with our adventures together.

At fifteen, surrendering my whole life and my whole heart meant the big picture, not the minutiae. After all, I could remember only four or maybe five of those fifteen years.

I imagined that Christianity was lived in broad strokes—as a highlight reel.

Minutes were what happened in between.

The house was quiet, exhaling after the tussles of the day.

I settled into my chair and heard the ominous creak of an upstairs bedroom door, the one that needed a shot of WD-40 that we never found the time to apply. Her feet were light and slippered on the stairs. I knew who it was before I saw her.

She said, "Mommy, every time I have a really happy day, I get really afraid afterward." She was ten, and she was thirty, afraid of the dark and self-aware enough to know the pattern of her fear.

We adopted our four oldest children from Africa, at various ages, though none still wore diapers when we held them for the first time. In two years, we multiplied from Nate and me to us plus four. As each child came into our fold, we had one thing in common: the ache of a life that felt out of time. They'd lost the innocence of childhood before they lost their first tooth, and Nate and I grew gray hair as we waited (not by choice) to grow our family.

In one sentence my daughter touched humanity's flitting response to joy: we don't know what to do with it. And our response to Him: we don't know what to do with His nearness, which reaches closer than our skin.

She didn't know about my wrestling with fear. After twelve years with an empty womb, I birthed a baby who threatened to incite more fear in his living than I experienced in the decade of wondering whether I would ever heal enough to carry him. After he was born, I asked in celebratory wonder, "Did this happen? Did I really birth this child?" Yet in the next breath, I feared that this would be the day that he might not wake up.

It was just like what I had done with her during the months after we'd adopted her. I'd stare at her vibrancy across the room, still unable to grasp that she was mine, only to fear losing her.

"Too good to be true" is humanity's response to God's gifts and to the God who doesn't just hold the files of our lives but also writes them. And studies them.

What I told my little girl that night was no different from what I'd barely grasped myself: adore Him here.

"The joy of the LORD is my strength," I told her, quoting Nehemiah 8:10, adding, "Don't focus on what you're afraid of, but look at God."

With each of our seven children—Lily, Hope, Eden, and Caleb, who came to us through adoption, and years later Bo, Virginia, and Charlotte, whom I held in my womb—fear haunted me. Three teenagers, a child in the in-between years, a five-year-old, a toddler, and a babe—all gave opportunity for fear. Fear is ignited in more than one life stage.

How many times had I shut the door to her room behind

me and unthinkingly given over to fear the one-minute walk to the kitchen? Dishes to do and phone calls to make and other children's needs to meet, forgetting what I didn't want to notice in the first place.

The unrecorded minutes for most of us are pregnant. We scrapbook our banner days—the weddings and births, first days of kindergarten and college—gliding over the significance of all that lies in between the annual family vacations. One middle minute can hold fears and insecurities and mind wanderings. No wonder we long for a highlight reel, for those banner days. But in the middle minutes, we discover who we are and what we carry.

We don't know what to do with the minutes in between, occupied by fear or boredom or aching—all the things we like to ignore and feel safe from when they are out of range. We overlook them, and we dismiss them. We develop eyes for the next big thing as an escape. All the while we miss the tender invitation, right there, in those minutes.

Giving our lives to God wasn't merely a broad-strokes yes for the shining times when His power is tangible.

He made us to fall in love during the middle minutes.

I met my friend Michelle for tea and told her pieces of my life about which there hadn't been time to share in passing conversations in the hallway. I was stretched with two children, yet unaware that the year ahead would include an adoption of two more. I loved the long-awaited early motherhood days, and yet I begrudged the loss of my time. The low-hanging cloud was my barrenness, still after nine years of marriage.

She saw what I hid, even from myself: cynicism and skepticism and a stalwart approach to my subtle and everyday ache. I gritted my teeth and endured, but she had another suggestion: fall in love.

"Have you tried adoration?" she asked.

Of course. Hadn't we all? ACTS, right? Just like supplication and thanksgiving and confession, adoration was somewhere in there. Like breathing, I was sure I had done it. Sometime.

She explained. This isn't a discipline; it's a simple way to talk to God. It's like everyday conversation with a friend. It's an engagement that can turn the hardened parts of the heart toward His Word and His person, expecting that He might soften them.

Adoration is choosing from God's Word a part of His character and His nature to meditate on, particularly one with which we wrestle. Adoration reaches beyond our thirty-minute, sanitized quiet time. It can come from our base questions and fears, our honest grappling.

But admitting the need to adore leads to a more significant hurdle: the need to wrestle.

Summer nights hold wonder for me after that summer following my first yes to Him. The light off our back porch filled in the shadows made by the moon's light as I spent night after night on the backyard swing poring over the pages of my Bible.

Those teenage nights didn't end at curfew; that's when they got started.

His Word felt alive, both in me and to me.

Every night was new. He was new, always. Parts of Him I didn't know made nighttime whispers, inviting me to explore them.

This was my version of summer love.

Not too long after, I made a type-A decision to highlight every verse I read in His Word in the hope that I might one day have that Bible all painted. My heart shifted as I filled those pages with florescence. I inched away from the freshness of a conversation with one I was fascinated to know—but barely knew—toward a routine as regular as brushing my teeth each day.

I approached my time with God as if it were less of an adventure and more of a task.

So how does one fall in love when the book is dusty or the God-man inside it reads like a historical figure or represents one more goal to meet?

Enter adoration.

Adoration is finding a pulse behind the Word and then saying that Word back to Him in our dialect. Adoration is asking Him to wrap His fingers around our dull hearts and to slowly revive them. It's admitting, *I barely know You, God.*

There are 1,440 minutes in a day. How many of them have I spent replaying old thoughts, reliving conversations, fretting over what was never mine to hold, and then at the end of it all, wondering where He was? How many of those minutes have I lived independent of Him, waiting for the next big moment of faith?

Adoration invites God into the grit of my life that irritates and exposes, the grit about which He already knows. Adoration is meeting God in the invisible, unaccounted-for minutes I ignore.

Adoration is falling in love, at odd times and in unexpected places.

Applying mascara.

Taking out the trash.

Pressing a bandaid against an obstinate wound.

Turning out the lights at night.

All the thoughts I have in those "insignificant" moments are ones He hears and knows. They tell my story even more than that highlight reel does, and He sees it all and desires to engage with me there.

When I adore, He slips off my watch, which demarcates the successful, efficient minutes, and He says, *Find My eyes for you, right here in the grit of your life.*

The minute-long walk across the threshold of my bedroom to the rowdy bunch outside is thick with invitation. I fill my mind with Him in that one minute. The wait at the doctor's office, the drive to the gym, the hours spent cutting vegetables and folding laundry and cleaning toilet bowls are all moments for adoration. He says, *Come, as you are, and I will show you who I am. Right here.*

To fall in love with Him, we need to see Him, to know what His eyes look like. His Word is our best informant, but it can feel like it's far from our days. We struggle to believe it.

I barely know You, God.

We want to tell the world what we know, yet the minutes of fear and insecurity and boredom and even downright nastiness can bring us to a place of confessional reprieve: *In the deep recesses of my heart, I don't really believe what Your Word says about You, God. Help my unbelief.*

Adoration exposes the grit of our lives to His engaging eyes, so that we see He receives us in our grit.

Everyone has one or more reasons to believe God is not good. Most hide them, unknowingly, until we can't anymore.

Some reasons may be like mine: body not working as it should, womb that remains empty.

Or parents die young, cancer claims a child. Money runs out, best friends find others. Marriages struggle behind drawn shades. Children don't always comply. Careers end abruptly, businesses fail. We aren't invited to serve a second term on the committee we love. Life is full of "not yets" and "didn't quite work outs" and circumstances that don't shine on a CV.

We hide our questions about God behind Christianese, right answers, and smiling masks. It's not hiding; it's a culture of existing that we have learned and now live.

Most of our questions surface in those hidden minutes.

I gripe my way down the stairs after a long day with loud littles, wondering if He is going to come through.

I spend twenty minutes scrolling through a screen before realizing that I'm looking for a way out of my insecurity as I face the enemy's accusations.

While doing laundry, I replay a conversation with a friend for the fifth time, still unsure how to navigate this conflict, still plagued by what I said and what I left unsaid.

I walk to the mailbox, silently ranting about a particular child's failings, unaware that my fear of what those failings might grow into is the cause of the rant. And I realize that I've never talked to Him about this fear.

Adoration is for the minutes that need a win, that need

His eye, His breath, His thoughts. Adoration is where I can come, raw and bruised, tepid and full of questions, and expect His response. All the minutes I've given to fears, insecurities, and inner woes I can now offer to Him for His interpretation.

Adoration takes my eyes off what I'm not and puts them on who He is at the very moment I decide I'm distasteful.

Adoration, beginning with one single minute, is where my grit meets His beauty. It's where the still rough and hardened places of my everyday living meet His person.

We all share the universal ache of wanting a wildly alive life in God and the challenge of reconciling it with hours spent doing the laundry, caring for a sick parent, and filing our taxes. Adoration infuses God into those middle minutes of paperwork and commutes and chopping onions for dinner. It invites the wild God into family rooms and kitchens, our interior spaces otherwise untouched by the divine. You can't receive God's tender, animated eyes on you in the drudgery and not revive. Adoration resuscitates the minutes we ignore and enables us to see God, within our reach, at 3:00 p.m. on a Wednesday afternoon.

Turn the page and consider what a few more minutes this week—given to looking up and recognizing that He is looking in—might do for your craving for Him.

Some might call this a micro practice, prayer in minimalism. Adoration is a slight shift in the minutes of the day that can move a life. Yours. And mine. In the pages ahead, I want to do more than hand you a map. I want to hold your hand and tell you my story so that when you begin practicing adoration, you will feel not only equipped but also emboldened.

The next five chapters prepare you for adoration, and the

thirty that follow those focus on the characteristics of God with which to adore Him. Read them over thirty days, thirty weeks, thirty months—whatever suits you best.

Shall we go together?

CHAPTER 2

THE POWER OF A MIDDLE MINUTE

Relearning What Is Radical

*One's mind runs back up the sunbeam to
the sun.*

—C. S. LEWIS, *LETTERS TO MALCOLM,
CHIEFLY ON PRAYER*

It was one of those days that turned into night and became morning without much respite. My sleeplessness was not because of a sick baby or a fearful toddler. I blame my mind.

The night before, I'd sat in a circle of women, our Bibles spread on our laps as we scribbled notes onto well-worn pages, studying Him together over hot tea and decaf. By most standards, these were the *safest* of friends, and I chose to let them see a little more of me. Some might even call it over-sharing. But depth of friendship requires that someone takes the first step.

Later, I wasn't as confident as I had imagined. My mind shamed me. "Too vulnerable, too premature," it said to me.

Hovering low that evening, my thoughts told me it would have been safer to refrain or to say it another way. The inertia of these thoughts continued through the night.

In the morning, I woke in a shame fog—my thoughts telling me what I'm not and all the ways I've failed.

Thoughts like this are sent to snare me. Identifying a thought doesn't mean I am free. I knew when I woke that morning that I woke up in a trap.

I said, "Help, God," and a phrase dropped into my mind in response: "The Word heals."

As my waking body untangled from the sheets and I became more alert to the day, I coached myself: *You know your way out of this trap.*

But I slumped back on the bed, grumpy. Knowing a way out rarely means *desiring* a way out.

I reached for my Bible and opened it to the verses I selected the month before for that day's adoration. "Let this mind be in you which was also in Christ Jesus, who, being in the form of God, did not consider it robbery to be equal with God, but made Himself of no reputation, taking the form of a bondservant, and coming in the likeness of men" (Phil. 2:5–7).

The words sat distant from me, my stubborn wall of resistance between us. I didn't feel the words as they echoed in my head. But experience made me stay in it.

"God, You emptied Yourself and made Yourself small, in human form, all so You could reach me," I said, without feeling, and then followed with, "I praise You for setting aside Your reputation."

As I said the words, I remembered last night. If stripped down to a mere sentence, it felt like an infringement upon my reputation. Sure, I desired safety and connectedness in friend-ship and was growing in vulnerability. But something about seeing the entire act of Jesus becoming a human described in the phrase "made Himself of no reputation" helped me to recall my reputation and my vigilance to protect it.

I whispered, "You came to be like me, so that You would know me." I needed to say it out loud. The stories my mind told me were not sustaining me. They were the age-old lines (for me): *Sara, you're too much for people. Too much emotion, too much thought, too much feeling. If you could simplify how much you tell them about you, then they wouldn't know.*

And, *If you let these women too close, they will leave. Close isn't pretty. You're better from far away.*

And (underneath it all), *You're disposable. If you don't handle these relationships and yourself within them well, what's good here will end. And all because of you.*

There were other thoughts, old thoughts presented as new, commingled in this narrative. Then, ever so slowly, I read the Word of God and spoke the Word of God and adored Him from that Word, and a flashlight shone on the torrent in my mind.

Torrent: not only less true than His Word but, in light of His Word, false.

"You took on the form of the lowest of humanity, just so You could reach me," I said with conviction. With tears. I needed a new way to see and think, and on this particular morning, I no longer read His Word like history, as one-dimensional. The Word was flesh. Near. It pulsed.

My thinking changed.

As I adored Him, my mind ambled around what was true. Though I wasn't living the reality of the women in this unique, sacred circle leaving me and rejecting our friend-ship, my mind took me there as if it were real.

How many scenarios that never happen do we live in our minds and feel the impact of in our frames? There are implications of these mental excursions. The enemy's breath can be hot in our minds.

For me that morning, I reoriented myself to what was true in ten minutes. This is adoration. Though it's not often this simple, what I experienced that morning-after was how He meets us in our insides, in the place of our dreams, dirt, and dust—if we let Him.

Adoration is where we bring our raw vulnerability—our "what I actually believe about You, God"—to the place of His truth, expecting Him to change us.

That morning I held no pretense. I set my bare thoughts before God, thoughts like, *You're disposable*, and, *Not made in the image of God*, and, *Capable of forever messing up a really good thing God gave you*. My thoughts don't hold up against His Word. When I pause to adore, they no longer rule me.

"That our idea of God corresponds as nearly as possible to the true being of God is of immense importance to us," writes A. W. Tozer. "Compared with our actual thoughts about Him, our creedal statements are of little consequence. Our real idea of God may lie buried under the rubbish of conventional religious notions."[1]

Adoration enables me to uncover my buried thoughts about God and apply them to His Word. Against the back-drop of my uncovered thoughts about Him, I put His Word in my mouth—His Words, back to Him, using my words—and my heart makes a slight shift. And then another. And another.

His Word heals.

In those few minutes of adoration, I brought my thoughts into alignment with Him. My mind cleared. My insides revived. And that morning, I worshiped not out of duty or discipline or Sunday regimen. I didn't check a box. I worshiped because of who He was to me in my weakness.

Adoration—seeing God rightly—produces worship. Radical worship.

I once saw "radical" as selling everything I owned or starting a ministry or adopting children from across the ocean. These days I'm redefining radical. I'm realizing that radical is sustained worship of God, against the grain of the world's distractions.

It's staying in the game, looking at Him when no one is looking or applauding, or promoting us for it. Keeping my heart hungry for God in the middle minutes is radical.

Adoration is fuel for radical. For being radical over a lifetime.

The four of our seven who were adopted wear stories that predate us. We missed many of their firsts and have years ahead to unpack what happened before they were on our watch.

One child's pain felt especially searing—for her and for me. Her question may have been, *How did these things happen under Your watch, God?* Mine was, *How are You going to heal this and restore her?* I slept on these questions.

The next morning, I stumbled out the door for my run, was back in for breakfast, went through the morning roundup, and finally, with arms full of laundry, that question answered itself, all in the unfettered swirling in my mind: *Her grief and yours, for her, is too big for a response. It's expansive, and you're small. Before long it will overtake you both.*

On that day, life distracted me from the swirling in my mind. The spilled hot chocolate on the mopped kitchen floor, the missing tennis shoe, and the teething toddler held my attention. They were things I could curse, fix, or cuddle.

It wasn't until hours later when I drove around the corner to a quiet space in our city, a worship community that hosts twenty-four-hour prayer and song, that I examined what was roiling in my mind. I was full of thoughts about what I'm not, where I've failed, and how we were living a life far too big for us to hold.

I walked up and down the aisle, listening to His Word sung over me. Choruses like, "Now to Him who is able to do exceedingly abundantly above all that we ask or think, according to the power that works in us, to Him be glory," from Ephesians 3, infiltrated my thinking.

Slowly, steadily, I thought less about all that I'm not—in light of this child's story. My thoughts danced around what He is, in passive adoration as I hummed along with the words in my head. Repeating truth, replacing lies that only minutes earlier had been truth to me. I started to see it all differently. My child is wounded; God is able. As unclear as I was on how to steward her story, He leads. God doesn't require of us perfection or knowledge. He wants us to lean into Him. And He is enough for us.

Adoration shifts our narrative to His.

That afternoon, the adoration was automatic, even verging on natural, because of years of engagement.

In the early days after my friend challenged me to

approach Him through adoration, this is what it looked like for me:

I would take a portion of Scripture—a phrase or a word—and tell God who He is according to that passage.

Using the chorus I heard that afternoon from Ephesians 3, it sounded something like this: "God, You can do exceedingly abundantly above all that I ask or think" (v. 20).

Most days when I adore, I speak one sentence and realize I bring a mind full of things that don't align with what His Word says. Adoration works the muscle of emotional integrity inside us. I can't get this close to His Word and persist with pretense if I want to grow. Adoration addresses integrity—honesty before God—at its core.

As I adore, I see, up close, the ways I have either refused to believe the truths I'm saying about Him, or have subtly accepted the opposite of those truths. I bring them into my conversation with this tender God, who knew all about my weak heart long before I told Him.

Staying with the example, my conversation with God tends to move toward this: "God, I have a hard time believing that You do more than I can ask. To be honest with You, I don't believe You'll even do what I ask. I'm afraid to ask and wait and not hear Your response."

We subtly resist admissions like this; instead, we form mental habits of dressing up for God as we do for church. It's the death of a child, the diagnosis of a parent's illness, or the loss of a job that finds us pounding the steering wheel in the silence of a night's long drive, telling God we don't believe Him.

But what about in response to the teenager we once weaned who now wants to talk back, or in response to the dearest friend who missed celebrating our big moment, or in response to the dishwasher that broke just before Christmas?

God is a gentleman, waiting for entrance. These middle-minute conversations make friends and comrades out of strangers. And most of the time, if we're honest, we approach God as if He is a familiar stranger, a neighbor whose presence is known. We notice when the neighbor's garage door is open or closed. We bring in their mail when they're on vacation and invite them over for dinner and birthday parties. We talk on the front lawn on slow Friday afternoons. But we certainly wouldn't invite them into the private parts of our lives.

To bring the fullness (or at least as much as we can see) of our inside wrestling into our dialogue with God takes our relationship into the places where we live. It enables us to see new angles of God in these new places.

For me, adoration oscillates between telling God who He is and admitting to Him the lies I've believed about Him (and about me).

I take my wrestling to this passage and say, "I praise You, God, that You work in exceeding abundance, even though I relate to You as if You operate in scarcity. I adore You for Your exceeding abundance in my life."

Sometimes I get personal and thankful—from my adoration—to weave the narrative of His Word into my everyday life: "God, You were abundant in how You moved in this child. I didn't ask for You to come into this situation with a friend in this way, yet You responded exceedingly beyond what I'd hoped."

The dialogue continues: I put His Word in my mouth, and I find my language begins to change. As I introduce the Word into my language, it serves as sandpaper against my faulty thinking.

Tim Keller says in his book on prayer, "We learn our prayer vocabulary the way children learn their vocabulary—that is, by getting immersed in language and then speaking it back."[2]

When I stay in the process of adoration, I learn a new language.

And as my language changes, my heart becomes inclined to follow.

One morning we stumbled into a language we now use every Sunday. I spent two hours coaxing four big bodies out of bed, clothing a toddler, feeding them all, then dressing and applying the rare makeup to my face and curl to my hair. I lived a day in those two hours and yet still felt as if I was minutes from my alarm.

Just as we made the last turn before the church parking lot, I remembered last week's service and the one before that. Sundays left us sleepy. And sometimes grumpy. Our children and I often experienced church in the same way.

So on this Sunday, I decided we all needed a new way to see this day. In an effort to give the children a plan for how to carry their hearts when they'd rather be in bed, I quoted a chorus from one of my favorite worship leaders:[3] "Sometimes you need to sing your way into the truth."

I said to them (but really to me), "There will be many days in your life that you won't feel the presence of God or the desire to read His Word. You won't want to talk to Him. If you wait until you feel like talking, you may miss the beauty of what He has for you in that moment. Sometimes you need to carve a way to Him with your words."

I'd seen this in my marriage. Pouring Nate's morning coffee, making his favorite meal, and letting him pick the restaurant for our date night on days when he annoyed me ushered me a bit closer to the kind of love that lingers past the early-married rush. I didn't do this at the expense of honest dialogue through conflict or expressions of hurt when he hurt me. They existed together.

I also saw this in my parenting. If I gave an extra measure of affection or a surprise gift to the child with whom I felt most frustrated, there was often a shift—in them *and* in me.

This is also the path I take into adoration. Sometimes you have to show up and sing your way into truth.

The best time to adore is when I don't feel like it, because adoration is not an exclusion of our emotions. Adoration never requires us to shut down our emotions. On the contrary, it invites us to bring them—*all* of them—to God. God does not want our polished pretenses. He wants our whole selves, and He wants us to come honestly. So He invites us to wrestle.

After an argument with my husband or on the front end of an unusually full day or when I set the phone down after receiving life-altering news, the very last thing I might choose to do is what has proven to scoot me closer into the most accurate understanding of who He is and who I am. I find truth when I sing, when I adore Him, from His Word.

Adoration isn't a new exercise regimen. It is not six weeks of Saturday boot camp. You are not merely adding a discipline. Instead, you are having a heart exchange that involves a conversation with God in His presence.

C. S. Lewis said it this way: "It is in the process of being worshiped that God communicates His presence to men."[4]

Adoration invites me into His presence. His Word, spoken from my mouth, and a reaching for Him (however weak) within my heart, open me up to receive His presence.

We are in a day of quick fixes—the rush of a caffeinated drink at three in the afternoon to interrupt our exhaustion, the mindless escape of scrolling our feed, or the fleeting but savory applause of others to what we post online. The quick reprieve is familiar, but I wonder if you feel its betrayal.

Our craving comes from a more profound need than a quick hit can satisfy. We want *God*. To be seen by Him, to be intimately known by Him—when one quick look of His awakens a dull part of our insides. We want to hear His affirmation at the end of a long day when all we see is failure. We want to feel His calloused hands around ours as our insecurities, once hidden within us, can now be seen by all. We want His palm on the small of our backs when the world tilts, even ever so subtly. We want the glint in His eye to be toward *us* when we're tired of what our shaming and scolding have produced within us.

Since before our lungs first heaved, He watched us. "My frame was not hidden from You, when I was made in secret, and skillfully wrought in the lowest parts of the earth" (Ps. 139:15).

And the rest of our lives on this side is an invitation to see those eyes, to feel their tenderness. To respond. Soft. Open.

I'm forty-one as I write these pages. At thirty-two, I lost my dad. In some of my weakest adult moments, I find myself daydreaming about when I was seventeen and got cut from the cheerleading squad and he wrapped me in his arms as if I was a lanky seven-year-old. Or when I was eleven and drowning in the emotions that often accompany middle school and he knelt beside my bed—his elbows near my pillow, his labored breathing close to my ear—talking to me about looking forward to the next thing.

Even in the years when my dad's physical pain kept him from being emotional stability to us kids, I reached for the nearness of my dad as an answer to both the big hurts and the little twinges of pain I felt every day.

His nearness was an answer. My dad was an answer just in himself.

God's nearness, His presence, is a response to our longing. He made us to watch us, to sit in His lap, to be His toothy, ticklish, wide-eyed children.

Adoration positions us to receive the sturdy presence of a father. (Even the father we never knew earthside.)

Adoration is a mysterious exchange. Some days as I adore, He arrests my heart with His nearness, His breath as close as my skin.

Adoration is not a downloadable workout plan or playbook but a multidimensional exchange between human flesh and the living God.

Most of us need awakening to the availability of this exchange.

What it can do for a moment.

And what it can do to make the interior life come alive.

CHAPTER 3

THE STORIED GOD

How His Word Heals
Our Stories

In your strings is hid a music that no hand
    hath e'er let fall,
In your soul is sealed a pleasure that you
    have not known at all;
Pleasure subtle as your spirit, strange and
    slender as your frame,
Fiercer than the pain that folds you, softer
    than your sorrow's name.

—G. K. CHESTERTON, "THE STRANGE MUSIC"

The house held a rare quiet as Lily, Hope, and Eden slept late, Caleb read in his bed, and Bo lingered in and out of wakefulness. The distant noise of ocean waves from the noisemaker that filled Virginia's room upstairs was the only sound I heard.

It seemed peaceful, yet I woke empty. The quieting of the daily noise made me notice my uneasiness.

Since the early years of cramming too much into my

schedule, I grew to know that the internal quiet isn't to be feared but to be explored, examined, and even pursued.

I sat as still as I could in my discomfort and listened. Not first to Him but to what I was ignoring:

- Days of passively assessing children's hearts and assigning long-term fearful expectations.
- Days of muttering, under my breath and in my head, about how no single person could handle all I had to manage.
- Days of feeling bad about me and thus being silent before God, sliding right back into my old way of believing that good behavior precedes good conversation with God and that a daughter needs to earn her hearing.

As I untangled this jumble of thoughts before Him, the emptiness lifted. I realized in the quiet that I had a lot to discuss with God. I needed the reminder that murky thoughts don't create a barrier between God and me; they connect us.

The pace of life can enslave us. Our humanity makes us vulnerable to the enslaving. We feel the distance between who He is and what we are in our sin, selfishness, and frailty. We don't want to be vulnerable and feel uncomfortable in our weakness. We scramble. We hustle. It all feels necessary. How else do we keep the pace?

The pace for me includes seven kids, my schedule full with family rhythms, piano lessons, mother-daughter dates, and so many mouths to feed.

For you, is it the boss's expectations of her employees or the overtime to cope with unrelenting bills or the 4.0 that ever-so-slightly evades you or the ministry opportunities that never sleep? Or even the "inevitable" fear of missing out that keeps your phone in your pocket and your social calendar full?

We invite God into our already established pace of life, give Him a small margin in which to speak and move and interact with us in the structure of our days, and then wonder why the rare quiet feels scary. And we feel vulnerable.

But we still carry a God-given craving for more—more of Him—and for deeper interactions with a God who can change us and soften us.

We engage with God at the familiar level and feel the void. You may be reading this book after mornings like the one I described, when you feel the odd juxtaposition of your discomfort with your quiet and a desire for more of Him.

"As Christians, we often feel the undergrounded restlessness of our ontological lightness even in our prayers. We find ourselves praying for God to 'do' this, or for him to help us 'do' that. Our prayers seem to originate from somewhere near the surface of our skin rather than any deep place inside. We go away feeling that we have not communed, that we have not put down our burdens, and indeed, we haven't."[5]

Adoration is one response to that restlessness.

It's a way to invite Him beneath our skin into the scary-vague empty places. Adoration isn't pious; it is vulnerability in action. In adoration, we start with the weak place, the empty place, the uncomfortable place and invite God to speak into it.

And we speak back to Him. Until the uncomfortable, empty places start to feel less daunting, more accessible to our maker.

Every day I make choices that determine whether I grow or stall. Whose line about my life will I believe? Whose narrative will set my course?

It often looks like this: the child we adopted from a hard place has a meltdown—her heart giving way, again, to the weight of years of loss and pain—and my inner conversation can go one of two ways. (And most times this is subtle.)

I think, *This pain is a carryover from yesterday. It looks like this ache may never lift. I should brace myself for decades of this.*

Or, *God has her on a path. Today is rough, but it is part of His healing her heart. He is making her whole, and today happens to be on the harder side of whole. It hurts me, and it hurts her, but I will lean into Him, here.*

We work hard to avoid our vulnerability. The car gets totaled, disease invades someone close to us, the business's sales slow, our babies don't sleep through the night, and our teenagers fumble and fall as they grow into early adulthood. We live vulnerable, subject to the world outside of what we can control, though we work hard to avoid it.

My life is shaped by how I respond when I feel exposed.

By putting on flesh, Jesus subjected Himself to the same vulnerability that courses through the rest of us daily. Hourly.

He "made Himself of no reputation, taking the form of a bondservant, and coming in the likeness of men. And being found in appearance as a man, He humbled Himself and became obedient to the point of death, even the death of the cross" (Phil. 2:7–8).

Our likeness is vulnerable. Frail. We sweat and cry and crack our skin open when we fall. He encased us in weakness.

And His choice to also wear weakness gives us an opportunity for a response when circumstances coax us into the false narrative that if we were bigger, stronger, better at bracing ourselves for the worst, smart enough to evade it, then the weakness wouldn't feel so terrible.

Jesus clothes Himself in weakness—He did not evade temptation—but He showed us what to do with it.

"Then Jesus, being filled with the Holy Spirit, returned from the Jordan and was led by the Spirit into the wilderness, being tempted for forty days by the devil" (Luke 4:1–2).

Satan enticed Jesus, after his forty days of hunger, toward power and physical reprieve. Satan hurled seething accusations at Him and offered Him a way out of them. (Sound familiar?)

And Jesus responded, three times, with this: "It is written."

In the raw vulnerability that temptation surfaces, Jesus pointed to the Word.

Jesus is God. He lived God's narrative, and yet He clung to the Word as His response to the enemy's suggestions for circumventing weakness.

Jesus' enemy was as real as ours, alighting upon our circumstances, adding weight and confusion to everyday struggles. Revelation calls him the "accuser of our brethren" and says he makes accusations "day and night" (Rev. 12:10). Just as he did with Jesus, Satan capitalizes during the minutes of our day to hurl accusations into our already swirling minds.

With the enemy in our ear, our minds need relief.

The Word is an agent of healing that we in our vulnerability need.

And what I heard that morning, in those dawn-breaking hours, was, "The Word heals."

Sometimes, it feels as if my dad died yesterday. Or rather, wasn't it yesterday that I hit tennis balls against the garage and he instructed my strokes? I can feel his frame against my back, training my arms to perform a forehand stroke. But when I close my eyes for a second, he is gone.

Grief is sneaky.

Like bells on a string, one small hurt hurls the next into motion, and the next, until discord chimes inside of me.

I remembered my dad for a minute. Then my friend and mentor Claire, who died years later. Then a friend, Mara. Life, called death, took them too early by my standards. Their stories weighed on me, and all the hurt, running together, sent me into despair.

I heard Nate's voice in my head, saying what he says when I get caught in familiar despair: *Adore, Sara. Do what you know will relieve.*

Just as the quiet, dark morning held myriad tangled thoughts, so did my grief. One thought, tied to the next, tied to the next, tied to the next.

I reluctantly opened my Bible to the verse I'd selected a month before as that particular day's adoration: "Return to your rest, O my soul, for the LORD has dealt bountifully with you" (Ps. 116:7).

I didn't feel any bounty. I felt the void of three lives that once sat at my kitchen table and listened to my life questions and knew my secret triumphs. The sense of loss hemorrhaged into expectancy of future losses; it preceded dread. I moved from grief to dread and stared into the Word of God that magnified it.

God is rest and is bounty. I was caving under dread and lack.

I started my adoration there. I, the little girl standing on the sun-scorched pavement with a tennis racket in her hand, bare feet burning from the heat, and the safety of Daddy's arms fleeting in light of what I know now.

It went like this: *I feel lack, but You say You are bounty for me.*

I feel the loss of life and the loss of potential and the dread that entered when my world turned upside down, but You say I can rest.

I feel vigilant and self-protective. I feel the need to guard against dread as a constant surveillance. I'm scared and lonely, but You meet me there.

I adore You, God. You promise me rest, especially when I feel fearful. I adore You for putting my soul at peace with the bounty of Your safety and Your protection. I adore You for the future You have for me of bounty, even though I so often expect lack.

As I pray from my weakest and lowest place, I feel His presence entering into what is mine to guard. I become aware that I am not alone.

Adoration isn't an evasion of my deepest feelings in order to placate the pain in discipline. Adoration is where I bring my most vulnerable self to the feet of the safe God. In adoration, I try out what it feels like to be fully me in front of all that He is and it frees me. On living freely, author Eugene Peterson writes, "The ability to reason in relation to what is in our lives, to assemble all the evidence, visible and invisible, so that we can compare what is happening now with what happened last year, to hold what we experience with our senses in relation to what we receive by promise, to read Scripture accurately and our own hearts honestly is essential to living freely."[6]

Adoration can be a bridge between our vulnerability and the gently prodding presence of the God who sent us His Son, encased in vulnerability.

C. S. Lewis writes, "We shall not be able to adore God on the highest occasions if we have learned no habit of doing so on the lowest."[7]

Vulnerability is the practice ground for adoration. We start with the weak places, the lowest places.

Pastor Tim Keller writes, "Another reason for the primacy of praise is that it has such power to heal what is wrong with us and create inner spiritual health."[8]

Adoration is an initiator of healing.

She lived a short time with us before I noticed the pattern. She was taller than most her age and a head above her siblings; it was natural that new friends or acquaintances, bridging a gap in the silence of conversation or looking to engage, said to her, "Wow, you sure are tall."

Every time she heard these words, she looked down and away. For hours and sometimes days, she got lost in her head. Shoulders slumped, she retreated behind her eyes, alone and shamed.

This happened so often that I anticipated when someone might mention that she was tall and, to stop this tailspinning in her head before it started, I changed the conversation or diverted her from being the center of attention.

Except one day, I couldn't. The usher at church gave what he thought was a compliment, and within seconds we lost her.

Hours later, after church, I found her. And she found herself. This time she was willing to eke out words. I helped her unpack her feelings when someone said she was tall, and after much coercion, she admitted that "tall" meant "not part of our family." Nate is six feet tall, and I'm five foot five. Our other children are average height. The mention of height, outside of the norm, translated in her formerly orphaned brain to "outside of this family."

The cloud that rested on her when she heard those words—the retreating, the anger—reflected more than the eye could assess. One harmless observation became harmful to one already harmed by significant loss.

It is easier to see in my children who were adopted than it is in everyday life: the way our history informs our thinking, living, and seeing. Most of the time this happens subconsciously.

Is there a phrase, suggestion, or scenario that, when it happens, sends you spinning? In a flash, you are in a whirlwind of thought, emotion, and angst that eventually lifts. Until the next time.

A new friend experienced an unexpected crisis, and I felt a nudge to care for her in a way that would bring both financial and circumstantial lifting. As I did so, she retreated. She barely acknowledged the gift, and as she did, anger brooded behind her eyes. She stumped me. Had I hurt her by this help?

Later I learned from her that friendship in the form of help felt not just uncomfortable but shameful. Her thinking was, *How can I ever repay this? I don't deserve this, and now I'm indebted.* More than these thoughts was a story that predated me and my offer to help.

What I saw in her and my daughter is the same pattern I see in myself as I engage with my history.

For me, it looks like this: my home with, then, five children was loud. My people aren't all neat. On any given day you might find the railing dislodged from the stairs, or paint from the latest art project pooling under the table, or disparate socks left under the couch. As much as I love order and work toward it, having this many bodies under one roof means that what was done is frequently being undone.

One afternoon a friend and her husband came by for a quick visit. Later she mentioned, through laughter, how her husband didn't quite know how to handle all the noise. She used the word *chaos*. A simple, fun-loving observation that most people would receive with open arms sent me spinning.

That night, I replayed the phrase in my head as I cleaned the kitchen and changed the laundry to be ready for the morning folding. I spoke tersely to my son when he left Legos on the floor after cleaning up, and I stood at the doorway to my daughter's room to ensure that her cleanup was thorough that night. I crawled into bed feeling downtrodden. Sunk.

"I'm just overwhelmed," I complained to Nate. It was a phrase I had used before, and this day didn't look different from yesterday or the day before when I'd felt invigorated. I had used the word *alive* to describe the day before.

Except.

Except that one comment, one trigger. My friend's husband associated my home with what he said was chaos. That one remark made a typical day of extra Legos, untidy bedrooms, and noise overwhelming.

This word—chaos—held so many other words inside it.

This word touched history—a history snowballing inside me, unhealed, and needing the healing breath of God to defuse its power.

Decades before, my young world turned into chaos. My dad—my hero, coach, and friend—incurred a back injury that left him wheelchair bound and sleeping on a bed in our family room for the first few months of my freshman year of high school. Years later, I labeled it a blip on the map. My dad went from fully capable to disabled. It was hard, but I still went to homecoming. I still got straight A's, dated boys, and made the cheerleading squad. I felt terrible for my dad, but it didn't impact me.

Or did it?

That same year my personality shifted in a way I didn't notice until I assessed my story decades later. My dad was injured and I cleaned my room. I went from a creative, opportunistic dreamer who never saw the floor of her bedroom beneath piles of clothes to a type-A straight-A student who got angry at disorganized drawers. I scheduled my days in minutes, not hours. I exchanged fun for an extreme version of responsibility. Dating boys and going to homecoming masked the differences in my behavior. I wore my cheerleading uniform over a churning heart.

My dad's injury translated into chaos for my teenage self, and I did my best to ensure that chaos would not encroach on any other part of my life. As his doctor appointments and surgeries continued, I clutched, managed, and controlled what was within reach.

Fast-forward twenty years. That mention of chaos in my home reverted me to cleaning, tasking, and scheduling. Chaos meant pain and disruption. Messy corners of my schedule were minuscule compared with the messy corners of my scared heart.

My daughter's tall is my chaos—both move us from logical thinking to emotional reacting. Both imply that we are subject to the whims of the heart, inevitably affected by broken parts of our stories.

We often feel fine until someone says or does something to send us to that "crazy place," that state of mental paralysis where we react and respond to what hurts in an uncalculated, unthinking, but familiar way.

We live as if our present reality is our only reality, but God has seen us since the beginning of time.

"My frame was not hidden from You, when I was made in secret, and skillfully wrought in the lowest parts of the earth" (Ps. 139:15).

He saw you when you skinned your knee the first time you rode your bike with the streamered handlebars around the block. He saw your first kiss and your first goal in soccer. He was present the night your dad left your mom. He watched you give your student council speech in ninth grade. He went before you on your first babysitting job.

"Where can I go from Your Spirit? Or where can I flee from Your presence? If I ascend into heaven, You are there; if I make my bed in hell, behold, You are there. If I take the wings of the morning, and dwell in the uttermost parts of the sea, even there Your hand shall lead me, and Your right hand shall hold me" (Ps. 139:7–10).

He witnesses every single one of our minutes, and yet we live as if this moment is the one that matters most in the making of us.

In God's mercy, our "crazy places" reveal fissures that

need His tending. The usher who called my daughter tall unlocked a conversation that led us into the deeper part of her heart. God used my friend's husband, who called my home chaotic, to reach me.

God is writing a story in us, and we find our place in His story intertwined with our discovery of Him.

John Calvin writes, "Nearly the whole of sacred doctrine consists in these two parts: knowledge of God and of ourselves."[9]

"So God created man in His own image; in the image of God He created him" (Gen. 1:27).

He made me to reflect Him, and as I begin to explore more of His character, His nature, and His way with me, His daughter, I get acquainted with myself. My story holds gridlines, purpose, glory, and even healing as I see it through His eyes.

But I can't explore what He sees without exploring Him. I can't see with His eyes until I nervously, shyly learn to look into them.

Adoration isn't looking at God; it is looking into Him. It is training my eyes to see His eyes, His heart, His way. Adoration introduces the healing of His Word and His Spirit.

Isaiah 42:16 says, "I will bring the blind by a way they did not know; I will lead them in paths they have not known. I will make darkness light before them, and crooked places straight."

Through His Word and His Spirit, I learn to see. My story gains context. It finds anchoring in Him. I see the aches, pains, and bumps in the road as opportunities to receive His breath, His perspective, His understanding, His healing.

Our God is a storied God, and I am one of His stories.

Yes, me at fifteen covering over the pain of losing my dad to a disability. Me at forty watching the redemption of former orphans under my roof. Both are part of His story in me.

Adoration invites me to come with the whole of my story, hopeful He will breathe life into it. All of it. Not just the easily told parts.

On the night I crawled into bed, grumbling again to Nate about being overwhelmed, any one of the elements of my day felt weighty—processing a child's history with her as she grieved, shopping for clothes with a kid who struggled with body image, orchestrating a birthday celebration for my extended family, and navigating another child's newly discovered learning disability. Yet adoration presents us with a choice. Would I choose to spiral, to wait out the mindless spinning and reacting—the head rush, increase in my pulse, and anxious scurrying and self-shaming and scolding—or would I choose to invite Him inside?

That next morning, I chose to step out of the spiral.

I slowed. I paused. I got out of bed and sat before God in the quiet. I asked Him to quiet my heart and tell me about Himself and myself. I held out full hands.

Aware that my mind was playing tricks, I picked up the Word to lead me. I read, "My soul [longs] for Your salvation, but I hope in Your word" (Ps. 119:81). I still felt irritated, on edge. One read-through of His Word didn't sink deep.

I emptied my hands and put His words in my mouth and my story. I told God what He already knew. *God, my soul is starving. I feel out of control, as if I cannot get a handle on my life. This chaos feels overwhelming to me. I didn't diagnose this as chaos until someone noted it, and now that he said it out loud, I feel sunk.*

My adoration started in my vulnerable place, giving a name to what was going on.

I moved on: *But You save. You are my salvation. You save me from me. You save me from what feels like a broken story. You save even the fifteen-year-old me from what felt like too much for her little frame to handle.*

I adored and I breathed, letting His Word sink into the places I had worked hard to cover and fix.

As I adored, I told my soul what was true. I felt the first lifting. My chaos was too big for me, but it wasn't too big for Him. It wasn't mine to hold but His to save.

You are my only hope. I moved on through the verse. *I can't hope in my order. Or my schedule. Or my management. It's only You. Your Word tells me what's true. Your Word never changes, even when my world tilts. Your Word is the hope that will never change when all feels like it's spinning out of control.*

This exchange worked His Word and His Spirit through my thinking and reached my heart. I started to believe His Word more than my fight-or-flight impulses.

Days later I heard another reference to chaos applied to my life with five kids by a mother of two who couldn't imagine all I "must face in a day." This time I didn't spin. He had carved a pathway for me in adoration. This word wasn't the end of me anymore. It was the beginning of Him—in me.

Adoration heals our insides and intercepts our stories, even our histories long past.

Pastor Ray Ortlund said in his book *Proverbs: Wisdom That Works,* "But we do not change for the better by turning inward. We change as we turn outward and upward to the Lord with an awakened sense of this sheer reality, his moral beauty, his eternal grandeur, infinitely above us but relevant to us."[10]

Adoration rewrites Him into our narrative—He who was there all along. When we enter it from the low place of our everyday reality and our story—our history—and look to Him, we permit a new way of relating to Him and to the world.

And the Word begins to heal.

CHAPTER 4

FROM THE INSIDE OUT

How Adoration Aligns Our Minds with His Thoughts

*As our senses present a landscape for
our body and its actions, so our thoughts
present the "lifescape" for our will and our
life as a whole.*

—DALLAS WILLARD, *RENOVATION OF THE HEART*

Sometimes it's not the searing pain that makes us forget that all of life is a story. Sometimes it's the slow drip of the mundane: another carpool run, another version of the same argument with our spouse, another trip to the dry cleaner's before Monday's flight, another rushed dinner after soccer practice.

And when you have twenty minutes of quiet and you forget that there is a bigger story and a bigger God, living through another person's highlight reel—gripping your phone as if it's the real answer—is easy.

It was a Saturday afternoon in early summer. Bo

constructed a Lego car in his bedroom with an audiobook playing in the background. Virginia slept deep, as did her teenage sisters. They'd returned to the age where naps appeal. Caleb waded through the creek with a fishing pole and nothing but hours ahead of him and the sun at his back.

Underneath the rhythmic beauty of our lives lay hearts that hurt. "People tell me they love adoption, Mom, and it bothers me," says one of my older children. "To me, adoption means pain and loss. I don't know if they realize that." Her self-awareness peels back the curtain on what many might see of our life.

On this Saturday, it all felt too much. The deep pain and the normal routine that collided in my kitchen. I didn't know it felt too much until thirty minutes after I'd picked up my phone to text a friend and got lost in a sea of other people's stories. I scrolled through glimpses of summer vacations and summer ambitions, past ideas and things I could or should be doing to make our children's lives more full. Guilt muted all other emotions. I thumbed through scenes that I once lived when we were childless—our newlywed friends in Europe—and remembered packing for a month across Europe with only a backpack. My mind flashed to the attic full of suitcases. Rest evaded me. An image of a garden dinner party came next, and I resented my weathered teak outdoor table.

A noise upstairs called me to attention. On the walk up, I came to my senses. Twenty minutes of living other people's stories all started because mine felt like too much, and too little, to live.

I returned to the quiet of my bedroom and considered the day—the hearts that ached, grieved, and churned, the toddler yearning for attention, the babe whose new word I missed. Together, they felt too much. I didn't know it, until my escape route failed me. My phone left me empty.

In those moments of feeling overwhelmed, various options invite me to escape the truth that God made me for something bright, real, and powerful. Many days those options feel easier than engaging the larger story.

And once it becomes an escape, we get derailed.

Some days, I would rather look at my friend and envy her hedge-trimmed life with three well-matched children, freshly painted walls, and soapstone countertops than address the part of my heart that started looking with that slant eye in the first place.

When I choose to look away, at another, my Jesus turns plastic. I lose the present possibility of Jesus' reaching into my world and my day. I see Him in such a way that it doesn't seem natural to bring Him my real-life ache, dreams on hold, or even the droning on of another Monday.

When Jesus is plastic to us, we escape into another person's storyline, the one we wish we had, the one that we envy them for living, the one that seems brighter and bigger and more alluring than the sock bin waiting for us in the laundry room. Mindlessly. We escape mindlessly.

All while the pages of His Word speak phrases like "being filled" (Phil. 1:11) and "the riches of the glory of His inheritance" (Eph. 1:18) and "He gives power to the weak" (Isa. 40:29) and "is able to do exceedingly abundantly above all that we ask or think" (Eph. 3:20).

These don't reflect a plastic Jesus who keeps human beings at a distance.

These verses reflect what happens when we get honest

with Him (and ourselves) about what we feel in the moment and ask Him to show up.

These verses can become real through adoration.

We look at our days as a sum of time, but time is a poser.

One of the most intense battles of our lives is not against the clock but within our minds.

Last week, I slid out the door for a morning run after the forecast assured me of clear skies. Fifteen minutes in, I felt the mist. I pulled my earbuds out of my ears, turned off my podcast, and listened. Something about the dew on my face alerted all my senses toward those country roads. God felt near. He wasn't newly near, but I noticed Him there. I wanted God more than I wanted to get home on time.

I contrast this with a morning from an earlier stretch of life. I woke up late and stumbled out the door in my running shoes, frustrated, still replaying a conversation from the day before that unsettled me. My mind roiled throughout my run. When I arrived back home, still frenzied, I forgot the country road behind me. I saw the rest of the day through a blur.

Life isn't so binary as my memory—either good or bad, once immature, now a picture of wisdom. But the contrasted moments tell a story.

For years, my mind played these phrases back to me all throughout my day: "if only I had more time," "when I come up for air," "when I get it all done," and just plain "I'm overwhelmed."

On the run last week, I still had six kids—two of them under four and four of them coming to us from hard places—and a sundry of other responsibilities that included homeschooling, writing a book, and making a weekly grocery trip. (That last one is no small thing.) On the run from years ago, I had two kids, not yet school age. They ate like birds and I wasn't writing a book.

Those same phrases haunted me when I was twenty-two, with no person other than myself to feed and dress.

Time is a poser.

Yet we live as if time is our monarch and let our perception of its scarcity rule us.

In the last week, have you heard yourself say:

- "I couldn't get to that."
- "I feel overwhelmed."
- "I need to get this finished by . . ."
- "If I had more time I could . . ."
- "Kids, hurry! We're going to be late."

What if time is not a good overlord?

There is this other part of our lives that meets us in the morning and reaches across every single afternoon and through us when we've turned out the lights.

The reach of our thoughts is vast, and they define our souls.

Whether sick or on vacation or facing a full day with a full house or taking a full course load of college classes, fifty thousand thoughts pass through our minds in one day. And many (most, even?) do so unfettered. We alter our schedules and resent when it all doesn't fit. We chase sand through the hourglass, thinking that more minutes in a day equates thriving, and yet He tells us this: "And do not be conformed to this world, but be transformed *by the renewing of your mind,* that you may prove what is that good and acceptable and perfect will of God" (Rom. 12:2, emphasis added).

At fifteen, not being conformed to this world meant ditching the parties and the alcohol, going to Bible study, and dating only Christians. I didn't consider that the invitation was to let God breathe on the untouched places of me with His Word and His whisper. I didn't consider that in feeling His breath there, my life would expand and thrive.

A thriving life in God starts in the unseen.

The myth is urgency. The tyranny of time can rob my soul of its true home. Yet the clock never defines my capacity. Rather, my capacity is linked to my thought life.

What would it feel like for you to:

- engage in your six-year-old's birthday and be fully present, savoring this kid for who he is and not entertaining a dozen thoughts about what he isn't (or where you fail as his parent)?
- hear of a friend's major win in an area where you experienced a loss and celebrate your friend without the icky judgment?
- play on the floor with your toddler without thinking of a dozen things you are not doing (or a dozen ways to Instagram that moment)?
- walk past your mess of a kitchen to enjoy an hour outside?
- drive for longer than seven minutes in silence and talk to God and experience His nearness?

This is a small frame into the expansive, abundant life

in the middle minutes, and multitasking or sleeping an hour less doesn't get us there.

For some of us who have a habit of racing the clock, the new strategy is this: "For though we walk in the flesh, we do not war according to the flesh. For the weapons of our warfare are not carnal but mighty in God for pulling down strongholds, casting down arguments and every high thing that exalts itself against the knowledge of God, bringing every thought into captivity to the obedience of Christ" (2 Cor. 10:3–5).

Every thought.

Will she follow God when she graduates? Will he pass math class? Is that pain in my neck something more than just an ache?

Our thoughts reveal what limits our lives. The minutes we spend replaying conversations and arranging a way out of a conflict that hasn't yet happened, all while running errands, are revelatory.

But to take something captive, we need to notice it.

The battle within our minds and for our minds could be the most substantive battle of our days. No matter the season, His thoughts are available to us. And they expand. They grow and enhance and bring life—a sharp contrast to the lies we believe about our limitations.

Our minds are a battleground.

If we win here—or rather, see Him win here—imagine the possibilities.

Author Henri Nouwen tells this story: "Once, quite a few years ago I had the opportunity of meeting Mother Teresa of Calcutta. I was struggling with many things at the time and decided to use the occasion to ask Mother Teresa's advice.

As soon as we sat down I started explaining all my problems and difficulties—trying to convince her of how complicated it all was! When, after ten minutes of elaborate explanation, I finally became silent, Mother Teresa looked at me quietly and said: 'Well, when you spend one hour a day adoring your Lord and never do anything which you know is wrong . . . you will be fine!' When she said this, I realized, suddenly, that she had punctured my big balloon of self-complaints and pointed me far beyond myself to the place of real healing."[11]

Adoration—looking at God and dialoguing with God through His Word—invites a settling of the mind. An alignment.

The noise of life is often surreptitious, filling the cracks and crevices even of our quiet, making us forget the power of white space.

When we have white space, our minds are conditioned to fill it. Mostly uncomfortable with silence and the interaction with God that happens in that space, we make our minds battlefields. We fill them with our narratives, the familiar ones we rarely examine.

My child misbehaves in public in a way that draws attention, and it is hours into my day before I realize I spent time shaming myself for poor parenting.

I accidentally buy the ten-dollars-per-pound steak from the grocery store in a size that can feed our family of nine. Days later, well past when I can return store-bought meat, I realize my error when I look at our monthly grocery bill. I sink deeper inside the narrative that I am irresponsible and incapable. I can live for days within this story.

I let a friend down, and in the weeks before our next interaction, I chide myself for being disloyal and selfish. We see one another again, and I learn she didn't notice and didn't mind, and I lost weeks of mental energy replaying my failure.

Even for the ones who live more externally, less in their minds, the faculties that rest inside our heads are populated and driven by something. And for most of us, that something is not our Creator's thoughts.

This is what Paul says about our minds, "Let this mind be in you which was also in Christ Jesus" (Phil. 2:5).

He also says, "But we have the mind of Christ" (1 Cor. 2:16).

Yet I mostly see the distance between where I live and what God has given me—what is possible as a result of Jesus living within me. If I carried a stopwatch throughout my day and measured the minutes I gave to replaying conversations, fearing future outcomes, and shaming myself into better behavior, I suspect I might look at those two sentences from Paul and say, "No way."

God knows my thoughts. He says, "'My thoughts are not your thoughts, nor are your ways My ways,' says the LORD. 'For as the heavens are higher than the earth, so are My ways higher than your ways, and My thoughts than your thoughts'" (Isa. 55:8–9).

And yet the cross affords a way out of the riptide of our thinking. Because Jesus lives inside us, we can ask for His thoughts, these mysterious thoughts. We can search after His ways. We can receive what our practical minds, charged with broken histories, cannot give us. Though life on this earth still holds mystery, the swirl of thoughts that dance in our inner worlds and tell us our narratives do not have to drive us. With Jesus, the capacity of our minds expands.

This God-man touched the vile skin of a leper and brought healing. Jesus spoke one word to a demon that fled, wept with a castoff, and in the same day He communed with God, undistracted. He gifted His life, mind, and heart to us, embedded inside us. We barely access it.

When Paul says, "Pray *without ceasing*" (1 Thess. 5:17, emphasis added), or "Let us *continually* offer the sacrifice of praise to God" (Heb. 13:15, emphasis added), or when the psalmist says, "And *all that is within me*, bless His holy name!" (Ps. 103:1, emphasis added), we tend to dismiss it.

But we have the mind of Jesus. And the practice of adoration brings us into alignment with His thoughts.

Our history plus the enemy's lies, years of faulty thinking, and our Bible illiteracy encumber our minds more than we realize. We get inspired by a quick quotable phrase and overlook the deep drink we need of His Word.

But we have His mind and He is ready today to help us have that space in our lives to expand, grow, and carry far more than we do right now, but with great lightness.

We want a shift in our circumstances or relief in our schedules, and He continues to invite us back to the place that no one sees but from which our days are ordered and derived.

The rest we crave is within reach when the toddler and the babe both wake before dawn.

It's within reach when we get the call about the diagnosis.

It doesn't evade us when we get overlooked for the new project at work or our book proposal collects dust.

We can have it under a looming deadline.

It's available beside your mother-in-law's sickbed and in the car on the way to your sixth specialist appointment this month.

"In the school of adoration, the soul learns why the approach to every other goal had left it restless," Douglas Steere writes.[12]

A wandering mind produces a restless soul.

A soul at rest is a soul that knows a brush with God, that feels His tender gaze capturing the secret moments. Our minds are the earthside gatekeepers of those brushes with God.

When the toddler and the babe both wake before dawn, do I let the rush of fear that I have months of sleeplessness ahead of me inform my thinking, or do I look at Him to tell me what to think and what to see?

When the diagnosis is delivered, do I play and replay scenarios of a projected outcome in my mind—planning the funeral and deathbed words—or do I ask His thoughts about how to face sickness?

When the project collects dust, leaving me sidelined from the work I want to do, do I anticipate a stalled career or another career path, or do I fill my mind with the hope of His Words?

At every juncture of my life and my day I am given an opportunity to ask and respond, "What will I feed my soul? My thoughts or His?"

Adoration is not only reprieve from the mind spirals, it is the feast that my mind offers my soul.

Dallas Willard says it this way: "The ultimate freedom

we have as human beings is the power to select what we will allow or require our minds to dwell upon."[13]

Curt Thompson in his book *The Soul of Shame* says this: "We will be aware of (know) God, others and ourselves in the same manner as we experience God's awareness of us."[14]

What happens in the white spaces of our lives—what we think about ourselves and God while sitting in traffic, walking the dog, pacing the aisles of a grocery store—tells the story of what we think about how He sees us.

The frequent bickering between two of the children tells less of a story than my response does. They repent and I'm still irritated. *When are they going to stop this?* My comments toward them are revelatory. Underneath it all, I flinch when I sin again, wondering if God is frustrated and asking the same about me.

I judge a friend for what I deem to be a poor decision, and my judgment tells less about her and more about me. Apparently I'm waiting for Him to judge my missteps instead of waiting for Him to see and respond to my earnest heart.

His Word brings us back to what is true.

Not only does it tell a different story than our minds tell us but His Word tells the true story. Adoration enables me to come from my weakest state and give Him permission to access my mind. Adoration is an assent—I admit that my mind is a battlefield and that I desperately need a win. These admissions cause me to pick up a new habit, try a new approach, and relent from my defensive stance, just so I can see God, myself, and others accurately.

For many who shared their stories with me, adoration came after a slow but hefty realization that every day, we offer our minds to death, and that our minds will continue to move in that direction unless we approach our thinking and our seeing in another way.

Romans 8:5–6 says, "For those who live according to the flesh set their minds on the things of the flesh, but those who live according to the Spirit, the things of the Spirit. For to be carnally minded is death, but to be spiritually minded is life and peace."

This life is a war, and one of the greatest places of struggle is within our minds.

When I grew tired of expecting that merely living more days as a Christian translated into a vibrant internal life, adoration altered my insides. When I got desperate, adoration changed my life.

Jesus said this to his friend Peter, who thought of his own opinions and suggestions as harmless: "Get behind Me, Satan! You are an offense to Me, for you are not mindful of the things of God, but the things of men" (Matt. 16:23).

Jesus demonstrated passion about having His people think His thoughts.

Adoration is for the ones made vulnerable enough with their lives that they are willing to learn a new way—to reach for Him in a new way.

To think new thoughts. To let Him win in their minds.

CHAPTER 5

WE ARE WHAT
WE ADORE

How We Become
What We Behold

Ultimately we are what we adore.

—TIM KELLER, *PRAYER*

In my twenties, I developed an eye for other people's advantages. Those in my same stage of life—friends from college, neighbors living in their first home, coworkers—gave me a measuring point. The weekend of Nate's ten-year college reunion, we were surrounded by peers doing significant things with their lives, having babies, and basking in newly-wed bliss. Ministries had been ignited from their passions, children were toddling at their feet, and the air between these couples didn't seem as thick as the air between Nate and me when our stubborn worlds collided. (At least that's how it looked on the outside.)

I saw lack in me. Everywhere. My dad was suffering from

the insidious impacts of cancer, my womb sat dormant, the youth-ministry dreams of our twenties had fizzled, and the newlywed phase had evaded our eight-year-old marriage. My cynicism, the hardness of my heart, and my distant approach to God were all marks of comparison and lack.

Ten years later, almost to the day, Nate and I boarded a plane and flew to a cottage nestled at the base of the Blue Ridge Mountains for a three-day getaway that included a night celebrating the twenty-year anniversary of his college graduation. We almost canceled the trip at the last minute. It came on the tail end of six of the hardest months of our lives, and we weren't sure we could leave.

This time, the "hard" wasn't marriage strain, a barren womb, or the death of a ministry. Our four oldest, all once-adopted, were walking their own hard, processing the losses they incurred while their peers learned to ride bikes and played with sparklers on the Fourth of July and built sand-castles on summer vacations. And as any parent knows, the pain of your child weighs heavier than your own.

In the midst of this, we discovered I was pregnant with our seventh child. While my friends were launching their children, God deemed it best to give me another one in diapers. Once again, these ten years later, I was out of step with my peers.

Though my heart was filled with almost more love than I could stand, for my six now seven, we know the human story too often links love with pain. To love is to feel the pain of others, to open yourself to having your heart broken. That was the gravity I felt.

I will not defend it, but my impulse toward comparison reared up again.

Yet three days at the foot of the mountains, interspersed with visits with old friends in the same stage of life but with remarkably different circumstances, made my heart feel full. I celebrated these old friends—what they had, where He had led them. Our differences made me marvel at the uniqueness of God's hand. I spent mornings on the porch of our cottage looking up at the mountains and seeing Him across the pain, the loss, and all that came as a result.

I didn't put on a happy face; this was not a flash of pious joy. Over those ten years—most of them spent adoring God—I learned to see Him in the hues of my day. And seeing Him in the breakfast roundup, the overflowing laundry, and in the incessant demands of life made it easier to see Him when my story felt broken (when our children's stories revealed their brokenness), when circumstances surfaced pain, and when unexpected news came.

Adoration trained my eyes to see *Him* in all the minutes I had once ignored.

His Word spoke a better word over my life than my comparative analysis.

These verses in Romans always mystified me: "And not only that, but we also glory in tribulations, knowing that tribulation produces perseverance; and perseverance, character; and character, hope. Now hope does not disappoint, because the love of God has been poured out in our hearts by the Holy Spirit who was given to us" (Rom. 5:3–5).

I knew few who gloried when they got pressed—some, but not many. But the fruit of pressing and the love of God in His Word and by His Spirit that intercepted my heart through adoration was developing a notable perseverance, character, and hope in me.

His Word was right.

Our three days away, slated for hiking and poking around stores, got doused in days of rain. Apart from the college anniversary celebration, we spent most of our time on the porch of the cottage looking at the mountains through the mist. His creation gave the backdrop for His work in our lives—breathtaking views, remarkable yet masked beauty, monumental work. Adoration made it on the short list of gifts He gave to equip us.

Ten years between nearly identical weekends revealed the change in us. All those stories that didn't match ours—of people who had what we didn't—created muscle memory, reminding us to keep looking back at Him.

Adoration retrains the eye to behold.

And eventually, we become what we behold.

"She must be so grateful," the cashier said while weighing my onions. "What a gift you have given her."

I unloaded a second cart of groceries onto the conveyor belt as three people stood behind me in line. I didn't have time to correct the niceties spoken by this woman with her assumptions about the most painful part of my daughter's life.

At the time, our daughter was anything but grateful that we'd adopted her. And I don't blame her lack of gratitude on teenage angst. Adoption came after great loss. Adoption meant something had gone awry for her little-girl life. Something broke and we were the cast. Her pain superseded any sense of thankfulness for the mend.

Though I felt irritated by such casual statements, I still

had days I wanted to hear "thank you." Some days I wanted our children to understand that for a thirty-two-year-old (the age I was when we flew across the ocean to start our family) who hadn't quite reckoned with the aching parts of her own story to take on another's ache felt overwhelming, scary, and enveloping. Some days I wanted my teenagers to have the discernment of a sage as they looked at their stories, no matter how unrealistic that was.

Like many parents, when I see a gap in my child—a way that child doesn't see with clarity or respond with age-appropriate maturity—I want to patch it. On the days that desire a "thank you," I respond with coaching—frantically reacting as if my words will mobilize an army, lead a nation, mature a child.

But as I grow in Him and those days grow fewer, I see His way with us looks more like this:

Her heart is aching, but she doesn't have the capacity to say, "I hurt." Instead a fog rests on her. She broods, wearing her years of loss in one moment. In that same moment, my choice is to coach and teach or to circle around, to wrap her in the safety of love.

Instead of aspiring for her to reach up to where I am—I, with decades of processing my story and a handful of people who helped me to see His hand in it—I bend down. Reach low. I let her be a child in her big-girl skin, a child I can hold and love.

One Saturday, this meant spending hours at a discount store with her while she tried on hats, gloves, and shoes. (I'm among the few women who doesn't enjoy shopping.) Another evening it looked like watching the British version of *Pride and Prejudice* in my bed while we sipped peppermint tea.

And still another, we made a late-night ice cream run with the sunroof open. We had our mouths full of sweet. Little conversation.

Love reaches into where she is.

And yet, in our own stories, we are less forgiving. We coach ourselves into climbing higher, seeing Him with greater maturity, and we chide the parts of us that need to be held.

Could the alternative be this: Let Him draw near. Let Him bend low, awkwardly, against your understanding of a God and King. Reach in to you, right where you are, and speak to that moment, that space, the lower rung.

We begin adoration with a mind for what we can get from it; this is human nature.

For it to end as a magnification of the glory of God, from us and in us, it has to start this way. We say, "If God is for us, who can be against us?" (Rom. 8:31) and yet swipe broad strokes in our minds about what being "for us" means.

Being for you means that God cared about your six-year-old mouth full of teeth; He saw your loose tooth. And He cares about your son's doctor appointment tomorrow. He cared about your first ride without training wheels. He's invested in your decision about where your child should go to school. He saw you climbing out of the crib at two. And He's not frustrated with the rift you had with your brother-in-law; He's pained by it too. He cares that your dishwasher broke just before the big dinner party. And He has input into your next vacation.

He is near. He bends low, not only to save us but to live alongside us in the very same limits of our skin.

In *Desiring God*, John Piper writes, "But we have learned from the Bible . . . that God's interest is to magnify the fullness of his glory by spilling over in mercy to us. Therefore the pursuit of our interest and our happiness is never above God's, but always in God's."[15]

This mercy spilled over the seven-in-the-morning fire drill to the bus stop, the burned dinner, and the late rent check. This mercy is what makes our insides come alive. It makes a heart happy to see His eyes on us in the middle minutes of our lives. And when we adore from this place—yes, from the bus stop, at the kitchen stove, on the walk with our dog—and don't wait until we've climbed high enough to say lofty words to match the words of a God whose "thoughts are not [our] thoughts" (Isa. 55:8), the initially selfish pursuit takes a new shape.

Praise is best given from the place where I feel my great need, and I see His ability to respond, right there.

"You can't worship a Being you don't respect or trust," A. W. Tozer writes.[16] And yet so many of us push past our buried lack of trust in a fortified effort to worship.

He is patient enough to invite us back to the sacred first things, like learning to trust. And for me to trust, I need to open myself up to see and admit where I don't trust Him and initiate a conversation with Him right there.

The truth is, adoration starts with our lack—not just admitting it but inviting Him into that place.

It's here I find Him gentle, circling around me on my hardest day. His gentleness lifts my eyes up, and I learn the first step of becoming—beholding.

Adoration is most powerful when I start where I am.

"We're too familiar with God," A. W. Tozer writes.[17]

Most of us package, label, and codify the limitless God. Familiarity allows us to avoid vulnerability. We like praising the sides of God we already know and learning lessons as a way of the Christian life. We migrate toward sermons and podcasts as a means of growth, rather than toward the grit of life that irritates and exposes. Familiarity becomes the safe sheen between us and mystery.

But to worship God as great—truly great, the kind of great that has our hearts racing at the thought of Him, that leaves us wanting to be on our knees on the carpet because His expression in our lives feels too holy to stand under—we need to let Him into the sides we protect. We need to find Him in our weak places.

When I feel His calloused hands holding the parts of me that bleed and calming the parts of me that writhe under my circumstances, I can't help but want more of Him. When I sense His gentle, forgiving breath on my neck—His nearness—after I fail, I want more of Him.

Every craving in my life is met by God, but I don't know this until I expose the cravings and bring them to Him.

On a Tuesday evening, as the kids go to bed, I want peace in the house. I want books put away, the dishwasher loaded, and the counters wiped clean enough to run my hands across without sticking to honey. I crave order.

But underneath it all, I crave a God who can put His hand on my back, assure me that He leaves no detail unattended, and quell all the chaos on my insides despite the disarray on my outsides.

When I get the phone call that my sister has cancer and my hands go numb against the steering wheel, I crave health. I reach for answers, assurance, and solutions.

But underneath it all, I crave a God who will fight for and with me against all that threatens to harm me. I crave a vindicator, able to assure me of the life, beauty, and victory in Him.

We feel presumptuous adoring God from the place of our greatest need, and yet when I see God respond to the deepest cravings of my heart, it feels guttural to adore. This cyclical nature of God's meeting me in my humanity, then my responding with praise that I've *finally* been seen and known and responded to in my darkest places brings God great glory.

When I experience the infilling of a God who is not too big to care about my insecure thoughts on a routine morning run and is attentive and watchful, then adoration has the chance to become as natural as breathing.

Richard Foster writes, "Adoration is the spontaneous yearning of the heart to worship, honor, magnify, and bless God."[18]

The more I see God seeing me in the middle minutes, the more I want to adore. The more I know the nearness of His breath on my skin in the times I otherwise deem uneventful, the more I want to worship this God-man.

John 7:46 says, "No man ever spoke like this Man!"

This is the response of one willing to see God as unfamiliar.

When we invite God into the new spaces of our minds and the pockets of our day and the traces of unbelief in our hearts, we can't help but worship.

And in our adoration, initiated by our need, lack, and craving, we are invited into the uniquely human gift—we get to move the heart of God with our mouths.

I planned an afternoon to write in a quiet corner of our city. Often an idealist when it comes to this craft, I dream of writing with a panoramic view of Colorado aspens aflame in September or finding a quaint coffee shop covered in vines on a cobblestone alley to write my books.

I carved out several hours to slide away from the house and choose parts of my soul to disrobe and examine, but as life often does with our plans, I got derailed. In being there for my son to comfort him in one of his biggest fears—thunderstorms that hit just before his afternoon rest time—I lost dedicated writing time.

When I got started, I had only one hour to write at a long study table at our local college. "Is this even worth it?" I scowled.

I felt the tension of my flesh saying *crank* as if deputized by the clock. But the strength of one phrase gave me pause. *This isn't the mode in which I want to create.*

So I turned on worship music in an effort to revive myself. A few phrases into the chorus, I felt myself unfurling. He wasn't a proctor waiting to examine my work. His kingdom didn't hinge on what I produced in that hour. This day was about our exchange, and my writing was for Him. I sensed that merely being there, under His witness and watch, writing words that I could offer back to Him, moved His heart. The words of Zephaniah 3:17 came to me as I listened. "He will rejoice over you with singing." And I thought, *He enjoys this moment. He sings over me and over this minute. He enjoys . . . me. Me, not what I'm producing for Him.*

He reframed my time as an opportunity to see Him. I

came, weak, and instead of plowing through my agenda, I paused and adored as a natural response to an uncomfortable situation. My muscle memory brought me back to searching for God from the discomfort in my life. God purposed the points of discomfort for conversation.

"A cup of cold water is enough to produce tears in the eyes of God."[19]

One unproductive hour in my writing can stir the heart of God.

When my starting place of prayer is my selfish need that carries me to the feet of God to inquire, I find the one who responds to that need. I find deep satisfaction. I become one who fulfills the great longing of God. I become a worshiper, yes even when my starting place is my weakness, and I find the answer to my soul's greatest craving.

"And one of them, when he saw that he was healed, returned, and with a loud voice glorified God, and fell down on *his* face at His feet, giving Him thanks" (Luke 17:15–16).

He heals me with Himself, and as I allow the vulnerability that incites His healing hand to reach me, my life and mouth can't help but respond.

This is the cyclical nature of adoration: from my weak place I reach for His strength, and in the healing I receive from that tender strength, I offer Him the glory that moves His heart.

We often skip steps. We read the last page of the book to determine whether it's worth the read, rather than letting the rambling narrative teach us. We cobble together our college class load for what will enable the best career launch, rather than growing through our studies. We model ourselves after the boss's favorite employee, rather than growing into our role and bringing the strength of who we are to the job.

I do this with our children as well—anticipating the next season, forgetting that their current place is one to be cherished. Changing diapers will one day end. Carting children to their friends' houses will end.

As Christians, we know that our goal is to glorify God, yet most of us have no idea how to get there. So we pose. We do our best to mimic what we think it should look like and skip the steps that happen between now and then that make a woman out of a little girl.

Isaiah 61 is a passage I pray daily. A section of it says this:

> To give them beauty for ashes,
> The oil of joy for mourning,
> The garment of praise for the spirit of heaviness;
> That they may be called trees of righteousness,
> The planting of the LORD, that He may be glorified.
>
> —ISAIAH 61:3

We want to be those opulent trees, producing fruit in season and turning heads toward Him. But this fruit—His fruit—comes in the ash wearing, the mourning, the talking to Him about the spirit of heaviness. Though He can do it in an instant, the life cycle reveals that God orchestrates growth over time and seasons. Winter, spring, and summer are all necessary for fall's harvest.

Adoration is like the hand of God cupping our fingers

and leading us onto a growth path that takes time. It is the assurance of unrelenting friend-God beside us, a leadership that is not our own.

The tree outside your front window reveals the miraculous. The elements of harsh wind, beating rain, and months of snow and sunshine combine to produce the first sprig of green you see in spring. The buds on our magnolia tree still make me wonder at God—years of underground germination are reflected in one burst of fuchsia.

The slow internal growth that happens as we let our eyes be trained in adoration, as we let Him place His assuring hand around ours, *will* produce a bud. Dozens of buds. The more we look at Him, over time and in the middle minutes, the more we grow into the tree that reflects Him.

My ten-year span between parallel weekends gave me bookends to see that adoration will change not only my thinking but also my being.

Our lives are a vapor. In this flash of a moment that we live, we have an opportunity to bring Him praise. The praise coming from your life is like no other praise He will receive on this earth. You offer Him something with your life's praise that no other person can. Though perhaps it's not yet identified, I suspect this is what your insides crave most. He made you to crave this.

As we adore, we become what we behold. And in the becoming, we bring Him praise. Our unique life praise.

He made you for this.

There are numerous personal benefits to adoration.

I look at our children and my motherhood differently because I adore.

He continues to bring healing to my past, my history, as I adore.

Because I adore, my mind has more space now than when I was twenty and had oodles of time. My capacity has grown through adoration.

I like reading God's Word. I pick it up at odd times just because I want to.

Nate and I have a strategy for when we get the unexpected call or when the waters get rough. We know how to receive Him through His Word because of adoration.

Mondays feel less daunting. I can find Him in my kitchen because of adoration.

And the list goes on. And on.

In all these benefits, we cannot lose sight of the full picture of adoration, the one that some of us might not assent to, deep in our hearts, until we are sixty or seventy. Others have an immediate resounding yes after they read this line: He is deserving of our adoration.

God deserves praise.

The person of Jesus, ensconced in flesh, with eyes that see into our souls and rough-worn hands and smile lines on His face, deserves our praise.

The life He lived for you deserves your praise.

If we start with duty, we skip steps. We miss the journey of bleeding out before Him and letting Him replace that ache with joy over a long road. We miss experiencing Him cup our faces in His hands as we mourn. We miss the smile lines. But not to mention the end—that God deserves our praise—leaves adoration as merely a tool for internal growth.

And while I love the notable growth in my soul through adoration, this practice is incomplete without a God-man on the other side of it receiving what is His reward: my life of praise.

This is adoration. I become what He designed.

CHAPTER 6

TINY BEGINNINGS

The Power of Starting Where You Are

Begin where you are.

—C. S. LEWIS, *LETTERS TO MALCOLM,*
CHIEFLY ON PRAYER

F ive days after we cut the wedding cake, I felt the emptiness that comes from orienting your passions toward safety.

Young, more in heart than in age, we collapsed into our honeymoon, needing rest after months of ministry output and wedding planning. And checking boxes.

On our honeymoon, I laid by the pool with my Bible cracked open and my eyelids drooping shut. I could find more rest in sleep than in these pages. This book read like a history textbook to me. No story, no thrill—principles for good living, things to learn so you could reference them when needed, and perhaps others to memorize.

Though I knew parched living for months (maybe even years), the noise of life had covered up what was hollow in my heart.

Activity serves as a wonderful mask.

I allotted thirty minutes for my "quiet time," as I called it, but no more than an hour. I watched the clock. I didn't call this a dry obligation—a calendar item—but I treated it as such. To name it would mean admitting a problem with my version of Christianity, and I wasn't ready.

That first love was real—the one I found in my back yard, on the porch swing, the summer when I was fifteen—but I had to look over my shoulder now to access it. Memory was my best access to Him.

So how does one fall in love when the book is dusty or the God-man inside of it is a historical figure? Or in my case, those words are lost in the splendor of the color that represents achievement, man's grand effort. (If I read all the verses but know not their author, I have not known love.)

How many of those 1,440 minutes in a day do I spend replaying old thoughts, reliving conversations, fretting over how my situation might unravel or evaluating a moment that's already passed?

My calendar isn't the place where I can make space or find time; it's my mind that holds the margin. The nine hundred waking minutes I have today are all available. I can be present while playing peekaboo with a squealing one-year-old, listening to a teenager recount her morning, or staying attentive to a friend's emotions. I can talk to God while I deliver laundry or set the table, in breathlike prayers asking for His input and help. There is space here.

My inability to engage with God's Word throughout

my day has less to do with the amount of free time I have and more to do with how I see Him. Or how I see Him seeing me.

I can stir ground chuck and cut cucumbers for a salad, all while saying a simple prayer from a well-known psalm: "You are my shepherd, God. Shepherd me." Those words invite love to grow across more than my morning solitude, my bedtime prayers, or the time when I taught His Word to a roomful of women.

My mundanity is His, to draw forth awe.

And it starts with one minute. One minute can witness even the god-awful turning into God-filled awe.

Tiny phrases, a friend calls them. *Tiny prayers* is a favorite author's label.

The best of love's beginnings are tiny. Sometimes, to begin, we need humility to start small. Very small. We need to start with now when now isn't glorious, scheduled, or a box to check.

The best of love's beginnings happen in minutes, often minutes that start as boring.

"Begin where you are." I had thought one had to start by summoning up what we believe about the goodness and greatness of God, by thinking about creation and redemption, and "all the blessings of this life." You turned to the brook and once more splashed your burning face and hands in the little waterfall and said: "Why not begin with this?"

—C. S. Lewis[20]

Our lofty and prefabricated understandings of how we should relate to and engage with God encumber our ability to receive His invitation.

It's three o'clock in the afternoon. Two children nap in their rooms while the others are at a coffee shop. The house is quiet, but my heart is still racing from all it took to get it that way. I'm sweaty, with mascara smeared across my cheek from a needed, but unexpected, cry earlier in the day. It's the same cry I have every few months when I remember that as a minimalistic introvert who loves order, it can feel alarming to live with so many big personalities who like to save things.

Every part of my tired frame would like to escape by flipping through a magazine. I can't form a sentence, thus the thought of lighting a candle and journaling my deeper thoughts before God is unappealing.

And then I remember the words of C. S. Lewis: "Why not begin with this?"

Peanut butter smudges on my kitchen counter and raisins convening in the corners of my floor don't disqualify me from a meeting with God.

Our religious notions, coupled with a task-driven American experience of Christianity, often leave us overlooking the corners of our life that are opportune for communion.

Let me demystify the habit of adoration: It did, and still does, often start with mascara-stained cheeks, tired eyes, a walk to the mailbox. Here, and sprinkled into each of the following adoration chapters, I tell stories of how His Word and His whisper intersect the overlooked, underscheduled, and underestimated minutes of my day. I want to normalize it for you.

When normal and divine intersect, we realize He is

present in the middle of our honeymoons, after a fight with our spouses, and while we wait in the longest lines at the store. His holiness pulses in every humdrum moment. The encounters with God that happen when we wear running gear leave an impact. We said yes to Jesus because we believed Him to be the saving thrill and joy of every part of our lives, and yet we need reminding that He came for our three o'clock on a Wednesday afternoon.

I will show you some of those three o'clock minutes. I invite you to talk to God in your sweat, when you feel overworked and under-recognized but reach for something, anything to numb your tired mind.

Adoration is agile. Like a sip of warm tea on a winter morning, it thaws my insides and opens me up to God. But it also awakens my dull and prone-toward-numbness senses at four on a Friday afternoon. I can adore God while driving my girls to their babysitting job or scrubbing the baseboards.

Brother Lawrence said, "I'm in communion with God all the time. . . . The rules tell me that I have to take time off to go alone to pray, and I do, but such times do not differ any from my regular communion."[21]

At the moment, I type while Virginia's monitor pipes ocean sounds, while Bo recites lines from his favorite book as he builds Lego cars, and while Lily learns Spanish as she scrubs dishes. And I know I can find God right here.

Adoration is limber, bending and flexing with my life—much like this writing.

I prefer my adoring to be with a landscape view during

those quiet and dark morning hours. But those hours are only a small portion of a full life, a full day.

So I adore God in the basement of my dear friend's home, awaiting the footsteps and squeals of all of our children, housed under her roof the previous night. I adore on my sister's pullout couch as I visit her to help after surgery. I adore on the front porch of my in-laws' home while neighbors return from their morning run and head off to work. Some days, sprinklers, barking dogs, and lawn mowers are my overture. I once got lost in prayer, talking to God about Psalm 91 on a short flight. During a spring and summer of unexpected transition, I saw the buoyancy of adoration—still accessible when my cherished morning rhythm wasn't.

We often envision engagement with the Bible to be neat, easily summarized, and full of lessons. Adoration initiates a kind of engagement with God's Word that isn't so sanitized, but neither are our lives.

Richard Foster puts it this way: "We begin [adoration] right where we are in the nooks and crannies, the frustrations and fears, of ordinary life." And later, "We do not learn adoration on the grand-cosmic scale by centering on the grand and cosmic, at least not at first."[22]

The mind that anticipates perfect conditions in advance of the perfect encounter with God will either miss the everyday opportunity to intersect with Him or will subtly create a dynamic with God where we come clean and He meets us at our best. The aromatic candle, dusted coffee table, and glorious sunset as a backdrop are a gift, but rare if we expect to encounter God in our middle minutes.

Adoration happens best in the mess.

We returned from a post-Christmas celebration with family, across flat highways that stretched for hours, with new packages and memories of cousin fun. And influenza.

The first victim sat hunched in the back, moaning as she drifted in and out of sleep for our nine-hour road trip. Within days, our home transitioned into an infirmary—mattresses strewn across the upstairs hallway in a haphazard attempt to quarantine patients in their rooms.

Then we all became patients.

There are two times of the year that I love most: September and January. Fresh starts, built into the calendar, send me buying new pens and journals for writing. I skip through my days with new intentionality despite the many years of Octobers and Februaries, the months when best intentions are laid to rest.

Six, then ten, then fourteen days into January—the flu worked its way through my family, rhythms, and new-year intentions. It rubbed me raw.

Except, my history of unexpected stretches of time afforded me this sense: there had to be more to the flu than a heightened water bill from all the laundered sheets and the cracked skin on my knuckles from washing my hands one hundred times a day.

January exposed my insides.

Temperatures sank, but God granted my heart the opportunity to stay afloat. The long-trodden habit of adoration became instinctive for my heart. Out of habit, I recited His Word and thanked Him for being the one who renews (from Psalm 51:10) while I moved loads from washer to dryer.

Without much thought, my trips from one sick room to the next included less griping and more adoring. Phrases from His Word popped into my mind, even ones (especially ones) that revealed a different side of Him than what I'd experienced in all these sickened weeks. They alighted in my head as breathlike adorations, informing my experience more than what I saw in front of me.

I am prone to cynicism, bitterness, and comparison that makes enemies out of the best of friends when times get hard. But this time I didn't take slow drags of bitterness. I didn't sing and dance, but I more than barely survived.

God made me buoyant too.

The part of the story that made all the difference—and the part that continues to take the ordinary and pain-filled minutes and turn them into potential—is that I brought my emotions and my wrestling to the Word of God.

Read that again. It's counterintuitive to us Christians.

I brought my emotions and my wrestling to God.

Jesus did too. He used David's words in Psalm 22:1: "My God, My God, why have You forsaken Me?" (Mark 15:34).

Circumstances are the gifts that unearth buried anger, fear, and insecurity. And what we do with those emotions—in a single moment—determines our way, perhaps forever.

I felt the angst of having the flu turn January black and empty. I felt out of control, subject to the whims of this vaporous virus or the haunts of the enemy. (I didn't know which.) I felt angry with friends who started their year with the inertia that December 31 releases. I saw myself as invisible, running the infirmary for twelve, then fourteen, and finally twenty days out.

I had a history with those emotions. And in my history, I

learned that the way to contain them was not to stifle them but to bring them to the only place—the only person—with an answer.

My adoration often, if not always, started with those emotions.

Like this: *I feel alone and forgotten—by You and by my people. I mean, who has the flu, still, after this many days? I feel trapped in this house and overlooked.*

(Sigh.)

But You see me. You saw me when I felt this way, tending to my dad in the last months of his life and sleeping in my parents' basement as I stayed to relieve the load. You saw me when I had a broken ankle and spent months inside behind glass, watching the unfurling of beauty outside. You saw me in the months of incubation after our adoption, when no one knew what was happening under our roof. Your eyes watched every minute. You held me with those eyes.

Not one of my minutes goes unwitnessed by You, God.

Your Word says, "Where can I go from Your Spirit? Or where can I flee from Your presence? If I ascend into heaven, You are there; if I make my bed in hell, behold, You are there. If I take the wings of the morning, and dwell in the uttermost parts of the sea, even there Your hand shall lead me, and Your right hand shall hold me" (Ps. 139:7–10).

So I adore You from this place. I feel unknown, alone, and tired, but You see me and respond. Your hand leads me. Your right hand holds me. Yes, even though I might not feel it in this minute.

Adoration invites our entire history into the conversation with God. Just as I bring all of myself—my fears, insecurities, profound testimonies of God's movement, little-girl moments, and childhood dreams—into a new Bible study of which I'm a part or into a new friendship, I bring all of that into my conversation with God.

We dismiss starting where we are—in the muss of life and the swirling of our emotions—because our understanding of His willingness to engage with us where we are, and our history of having Him engage with us where we were (all the questions, insecurities, rampant fears that can course through a small person) is limited.

Adoration allows me to bring all of me—sighing, tears, frustrations, and anger—to Him and His Word and hope that I won't walk away the same.

Adoration went before me, instinctually, during all those flu-filled days.

"The vulnerability of nakedness is the antithesis of shame," Curt Thompson says in his book *The Soul of Shame*.[23] Bareness before God shows up in unexpected places, in the everyday chaos of life. The flu, the squabble with our spouse, the child who melted down at the worst moment, the delayed but promised payment.

In the middle minutes.

You're here because you're hungry. And not for a more disciplined, structured way to approach God. You are here for Him.

I suspect that on the other side of these thirty attributes of God by which to adore, the minutes between when you adore will change. More conversation in the middle minutes, more reaching to Him instead of the escapes, and more electricity in your heart toward God are all benefits of adoration. My life is less anxious and less boring and my mind is more full since I started adoring.

Ultimately, He receives more worship—more of me, fully alive and looking to Him and bringing Him glory. (Yes, the mess in the middle minutes can be the backdrop for glory.)

You came hungry, and I expect you will leave more aware that your much resisted neediness opens the door to vibrant strength and awe-producing beauty in His world.

Charles Spurgeon says, "Let us spread our adoration over all the day, till from the moment when we open our eyes till we close them again at night, we shall be practically worshipping the Lord."[24]

Paul pens this: "Pray without ceasing" (1 Thess. 5:17).

Adoration and prayer can feel vastly distant from the long list of responsibilities we wake to at six in the morning, the bills waiting in our mailboxes, and the argument we just had with our spouses, unless we see how readily accessible adoration is in both our best and worst minutes.

May the chapters ahead make the concept of adoration, often perceived to be lofty, applicable to your everyday grit. May these chapters be gentle but prodding and slightly instructive, with much room for individual creative license before God.

And at the end of inviting these thirty attributes of God to intersect with your life and your understanding of Him, my hope is that, in closing the pages of this book, you will be hungrier for Him and yet more satisfied by Him than you have ever been before.

For thirty days or three months or however long you choose, you have a guide through the attributes of God. Many of these may be sides of God you wrestle to believe, when you are honest.

Resist the urge to formalize, and instead use this approach to prayer in the way that suits this stretch of your life and your heart's questions.

IN THE GRIT

In each chapter, I highlight an attribute of God that—when I am quiet and honest—I admit I struggle to believe. I may teach it to our children or to myself, and yet when I experience delay or disappointment, my heart tells a different story.

I learn through story. In each chapter I tell you my stories, the ones where I skidded my knees against the pavement and lived what it's like to have Him bandage and soothe. I invite you in past the foyer into the family room, to see how adoration impacts the way I know God.

Because of space limitations, it may appear as if my life ache gets resolved in one story. Don't see this as simple, if my story appears simple. Every good story has pieces that only the author and the main character know and live. In between the lines of these stories are sleepless nights and sweaty palms. The best growth in God comes in the grit. I give you permission to read between the lines—the growth in adoration is sometimes cumbersome and long suffered and gritty.

AND HERE, IN THE MIDDLE MINUTES, WE ADORE

These sections are my creative response to God—for you to see. Left-brained, linear thinkers may choose to skip this portion. Others may find that it helps release creativity into your dialogue with God. And some of you may think you function out of your left brain, but find that a creative expression to God is exactly what you need to dislodge old ways of relating to Him.

Some days, adoration is under my breath, and I say it in breathlike prayers—those tiny prayers and phrases, not long but expressive. Other days, when there is a little more white space (or I reclaim a little more white space), I write out my adorations, just as I've done here. They are not the Word. They are not His words. They are simply my response.

SCRIPTURE LIST AND HOW TO USE IT

Next I provide you with verses that can stretch across minutes or days or months. These are not comprehensive lists. In this section, I put my hand around yours and walk you through the landscapes I traveled in the Word as I wrestled through each of these sides of God. Please add to this list—take new footpaths through the Bible as you walk this way and discover fresh things about Him.

I encourage you not only to read but also to adore through these. This section is not intended for an in-depth study (though you may find yourself studying as you go); these verses are your launch pad for adoration.

Some may want to stay in one characteristic for weeks. I adored through one psalm for an entire summer. Others may want to move along to the next in a day, with the potential of circling back later. Still others may bounce around, burying themselves in one particular characteristic on one day and starting fresh with another the next.

I selected these verses using the New King James Version

of the Bible. If your version is different, you may need to poke around in this one to see the connection to the attribute. I love toggling between different versions of the Bible to gain a fuller understanding of each verse.

For several years, January 1 has meant studying two to three new books of the Bible for the year. My friend Molly and I spend the weeks leading up to the new year compiling a resource list of commentaries and sermons and books on the texts we plan to study. We spend a year in these books of the Bible and end every year feeling as if we need another in this same book to dive deep.

But this is not that kind of study. Adoration is an invitation into a deeper study of the living God-man within the Word. Like me, many of you may have spent years on the front porch of the Bible or within one room. My hope for you, through this book, is that you will fall in love with the God-man who wrote it and His poetical, intimate words for the people He formed.

TINY (BIG) PRAYERS

A year into fumbling through life with four children (through adoption, we grew from zero to four children in two years), I found an asset in the one-sentence, one-phrase prayers.

For a while I tried the acrobatics of squeezing my life with four children into the framework I lived prior to them. But it didn't work. This is when I started praying tiny prayers. Simple prayers, but prayers I knew He heard.

Move her heart toward You, I prayed as I kissed her goodnight.

Help him to love when all he feels is pain, I prayed as I saw my son squirm under the ache of terse words from a sibling.

Give me enough for them for today, I muttered on a quick walk away from the breakfast table.

It wasn't long before I realized I could take these tiny prayers with me anywhere—in the waiting room at the dentist, during the unexpected traffic backup, in the hour of recital performances leading up to my child's turn. These tiny phrases helped me to offer big prayers in an accessible way, in tiny breathlike wisps.

In this section of the book, I give you a prayer-reach for that side of Him you are adoring directly from His Word. Steal them, then use and reuse them. Reach in the middle minutes, through these prayers.

DIALOGUE WITH HIM

Putting the barest parts of our insides close to His Word sparks new dialogue with God. When we feel discovered and uncovered, in safety, we lean in to what He might say to us. It's often surprising how gentle God is with the weak and masked parts of us.

These questions at the end of each chapter are an appeal to step away from seeing Him as a task or a means toward a desirable end, and toward seeing Him as a Father, ready to have you rest your head on His chest and sigh. And unfold.

And with this, I hand you the keys. Open the door and find new sight.

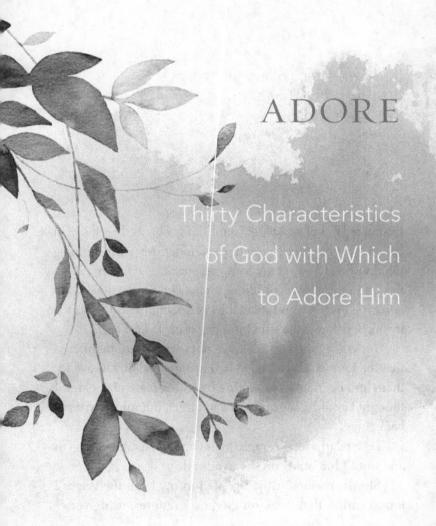

ADORE

Thirty Characteristics
of God with Which
to Adore Him

1 | RESTORER

Make me hear joy and gladness,
that the bones You have broken
may rejoice.

—PSALM 51:8

IN THE GRIT

I stumbled out of bed at 5:47 a.m. and got dressed for the gym before allowing myself time to reconsider. My early-morning mind works at a speed my body can't track, as if to remind me that only my limbs sleep. I thought about how to get my stiff fingers to tie my shoes and about the encroaching fears I'd courted the night before—the ones I was preparing to date again.

Yesterday was one of those days when I remembered that the four we had adopted had histories I didn't weave for them and heartaches I couldn't fix with a plate of cookies. I thought I could wake up fresh and forget, but my mind went back there.

I stayed in a fog through the seven-mile drive to the gym and until I hit "start" on the treadmill.

Slowly, methodically, I recited in my head the verses I found earlier that week on God as a restorer, using verses from the worn journal I propped open in front of me on the treadmill. The odometer read one mile. My recitation turned slowly toward a declaration: *Their insides bleed, Lord. Their bones are broken. Make them hear joy and gladness.* David's words in Psalm 51 were now mine.

I asked and I adored, intermingling conversation. I told Him and my weak heart what was true: *You make the darkened parts of their life hear joy. How could that be? But You do. I adore You for making broken bones sing.*

I felt myself—all of me—being received by Him, which opened me to receive these words back.

Moving from this verse on to the next and the next, my heart warmed along with my joints.

A few miles later, walking through my cooldown, I noted a shift. I felt an inkling of hope. *He restores?* Though still a question, I was asking it while assuming the answer.

His Spirit worked something in me. The words I sweat over lifted off the page and into me.

And it wasn't even 8:00 a.m. yet.

AND HERE, IN THE MIDDLE MINUTES, WE ADORE
USING PSALM 51:8

You restore.

And restoration answers. It sings.

It is the place where all the broken pieces receive a binding, a forever healing. You fuse loud discord— misplaced cries, fragmented storylines, aches of bones long broken—into one symphonic sound. And

I praise as You do it. Yes, I adore as You restore me, and I watch it all happening.

I find joy in You, God. Gladness is offered even to the most badly broken pieces of me. Right now.

You offer a wholeness to those who are shells of what they were intended to be. No one is too far gone. No, not even me.

Your restoration interrupts the dull and lifeless parts of me like a mourning dove: coo, coo, coo. You revive as You restore.

You interrupt the parts of me that are quieted by the pain of life, God, with Your restoration.

You are restoration, God. In Your personhood, in Your nearness, You restore.

I crave You, God. My broken body craves You. Every bone that aches because of my sin or someone else's sin or injustice receives a new song.

Today. Now. Even at 6:33 a.m.

You restore the unlikely, and I adore You as You restore and someplace deep within me starts to sing.

A joy I can't fake rattles within me when I look at You restoring me, because I realize there is a life ahead of me of watching like an unsophisticated child studies the mourning dove. Expectant.

I am made whole in You.

MY RESTORER

Deuteronomy 30:3 | Job 42:10 | Psalm 23:1–3 | Psalm 26:8, 11 | Psalm 34:18 | Psalm 51:8 | Psalm 61:6–7 | Psalm 69:18 | Psalm 71:20 | Psalm 80:3, 7, 19 | Psalm 113:7–9 | Psalm 130:7 | Psalm 147:3 | Isaiah 62:4 | Hosea 3:5 | Joel 2:25–26 | Matthew 11:28–30 | Luke 8:43–44 | 2 Corinthians 13:9b, 11a | Revelation 21:3–5

TINY (BIG) PRAYERS

"Make me hear joy and gladness" (Ps. 51:8).
"Redeem me" (Ps. 26:11).
"Restore my soul" (Ps. 23:3).

DIALOGUE WITH HIM

Who or what in your life—including yourself—do you have a hard time believing that He can restore?

As you adore Him this day or throughout this week, set aside a few minutes as often as you need (as often as it surfaces) to confess your struggle to believe that He can restore.

Ask Him, as you confess, to reveal what may be hindering your ability to believe that He is a restorer. (For those of you who love to write, talk to Him on the page. Ask your questions and leave space for His response. Keep your Bible cracked open. His Word holds answers, even—and especially—ones we have a hard time believing but with which we are invited to grapple.)

Toward the end of this stretch of adoration, take a few minutes at odd times of the day to pray that He will restore those parts of you or another that have seemed like they are at an impasse. Use "Tiny (BIG) Prayers" to inform your language if you need help.

As you see signs of His work here (yes, even small traces), praise. Adore again, with more belief to fuel your adoration. (And if you don't yet see signs of His work, don't be discouraged. The deepest rivers take time to cross. Keep adoring and fording.)

2 | THE GOD WHO SEES

The eyes of the LORD are in every place, keeping watch on the evil and the good.

—PROVERBS 15:3

IN THE GRIT

I stopped keeping a tally of the baby showers, much like some of my friends have stopped counting their bridesmaid dresses. A growing count of the times I felt invisible only worsened my mindset about my empty womb. Not only did baby showers remind me of what I didn't have but the sisterhood circle of conversation drew a divide, accidentally separating those who were in from those who were out. I knew enough to define words like *epidural* and *effaced* and *dilated*, but I was still out. Although I wanted to have everything to do with this club, my body (and some days, I thought, my God) excluded me. And so, on my harder days, I secretly disdained them—these who lived what I could only define.

One baby shower happened years into my waiting-room stay. The room held moms, newlyweds, and me. Curious new brides asked questions, and experienced moms were excited at the chance to share their knowledge. Finally, the expectant mother—pregnant with her third—spoke words I suspected were true but hoped no one would say in my hearing. I could not know or reach the connectedness to God into which her previous births seemed to usher her. Her emotive exuberance sent me to the dark place of my soul, asking, *Is there a place for me, God?* The power and beauty of her story left me feeling discarded—alone and unseen in my lack.

This vignette and a host of others amassed over time, drawing my vision, my perspective, and my hope inward and downward. Until something nudged me to consider His eyes.

I got lost in the couch pillows among the sisterhood of women with stretch marks, but I found in His Word that He saw me.

I slinked, invisible, into the shadowed corners of the fourth floor of Martha Jefferson Hospital where my friends birthed their babies until I discovered how His eyes saw those invisible minutes.

I felt discarded, carrying a barren womb in sight of another's growing girth, until I understood that His nearness to the brokenhearted means that He brought all of Himself into their pain. Even His eyes. He heals with His eyes, His sight into my pain.

Adoration bridged the gap between my heart and my mind during those long, barren years. My mind started to understand that He saw me in my invisibility when I felt discarded, as I walked with empty arms during the childbearing years. Adoration moved those truths from my mind into my heart.

As I adored the God who sees me, I started to feel seen.

I adored the God whose eyes witnessed my unformed frame, and I started to believe He witnessed my invisible heart.

As I adored the God who had more thoughts toward me than I had of my own, I became less scared of the thoughts inside my mind. I wanted to hand them over to Him and to receive His instead.

Adoration moved the Sunday school truth that God sees me into my daily understanding of myself. I continued to attend those baby showers.

AND HERE, IN THE MIDDLE MINUTES, WE ADORE

USING PROVERBS 15:3

God, You see me.

I once marveled at how You saw the earth before You formed it and man before You made his frame. I thought about how You saw the planets and galaxies—all the things beyond my seeing.

But it astounds me how You see my heart.

I adore You for examining the complexities within that I cannot name and often don't understand.

I adore You, God, that Your eyes did not miss one of my minutes. You see them all.

I praise You for seeing what I want to forget (and bringing me back there for Your healing) and for seeing all the overlooked parts of my life.

You don't miss one aspect of my life, not one single minute.

I adore You for being near me in my pigtails and when I tossed another negative pregnancy test into the trash and while I was at another baby shower.

Your seeing heals me. Your seeing me heals me. Your eyes, they see what I cannot. They mirror for my heart what I want to see.

I adore You for sharing Your eyesight with me, God.

GOD WHO SEES

Genesis 16:13 | Exodus 2:23–25; 3:7 | 2 Chronicles 16:9 | Psalm 1:6 | Psalm 10:14 | Psalm 11:4 | Psalm 32:8 | Psalm 33:13–15 | Psalm 139:1–2, 15, 16, 23 | Psalm 146:9 | Proverbs 5:21 | Proverbs 15:3 | Matthew 6:6 | Matthew 6:17–18 | Luke 7:36–50 | Hebrews 4:13

TINY (BIG) PRAYERS

"The eyes of the LORD are in every place" (Prov. 15:3).
"You-Are-the-God-Who-Sees" (Gen. 16:13).
"Your Father who sees in secret" (Matt. 6:6).

DIALOGUE WITH HIM

Identify two or three times in the last month when you felt unseen. Writing them out may enable you to explore them, since we tend to forget moments that elicit negative or unmanageable feelings. After you list these, note your response. How did you feel? What did you do as a result? Pay attention to your heart, considering those moments both now and as you lived them. Bring those feelings and your responses under the light of God's eyes.

There may need to be a break between when you note

the times when you felt unseen and when you invite God into them. You may need to "collect more data"—to remember, to let yourself feel again what you felt then. After you assess those unseen moments, take one to three of the verses listed in the "God Who Sees" section and write them out. As you write, ask Him to bring them off the page and into your heart.

With the memory in mind of when you felt unseen, adore who He is in His Word as the God who sees you. Let adoration bridge the gap between what you read from His Word and the times when you felt unseen. Invite His Holy Spirit to do what Hebrews 4:12 describes: "For the word of God is living and powerful, and sharper than any two-edged sword, piercing even to the division of soul and spirit, and of joints and marrow, and is a discerner of the thoughts and intents of the heart."

Invite Him in to discern your thoughts and to respond to what is on your insides—the ache of being unseen.

3 | MY STRENGTH

I will love You, O LORD, my strength. The LORD is my rock and my fortress and my deliverer; my God, my strength, in whom I will trust; my shield and the horn of my salvation, my stronghold. I will call upon the LORD, who is worthy to be praised; so shall I be saved from my enemies.

—PSALM 18:1–3

IN THE GRIT

At sixteen I needed God to give me endurance for exams week and strength for long days of after-school cheerleading tryouts. I felt weak when I got asked to prom by the wrong guy and when I didn't make student council my senior year of high school.

The later decades of my life included weaknesses for which I never prepared. But sometimes it's in returning to the small struggles when the truth gets forged.

One Sunday, a migraine came on, and I crawled under the covers hoping to sleep it off. I couldn't sleep, so I puttered around the house, putting away dishes and wiping the counters—doing anything to take my mind off the pain.

A Bible verse on a note card on the back of my kitchen

sink caught my eye. "The LORD is my rock and my fortress and my deliverer; my God, my strength" (Ps. 18:2).

Like any decorative staple, the verse I had set out on a motivated day was forgotten in the days that followed. Who knows how long it had been there, watermarked from the dish soap and spray, waiting for this day to remind me.

There was a strength, other than my own, available.

You are my strength when I am weak seems more natural to sing in a full room of other believers when I feel strong than when weakness has wrapped itself around my head.

I adored what I didn't believe, what I could barely say. Under my breath—without the strength to say the words out loud—I whispered, *You are my strength.*

I told my unbelieving heart and my stubborn body what was true. I chose weakness, instead of stalwart endurance. With my adoration, I chose neediness instead of human fortitude.

He was my strength when my dad died and during long years of infertility. The dark valleys left me no option but to reach for Him, for His strength, with a weak and trembling hand. But revealed in the small gut-it-out minutes is my inclination not to reach, not to need. And not to receive.

On this average Sunday, I felt Him carrying me in my weakness, my *familiar* weakness.

The familiar is often the enemy of our souls. How many migraines did I endure before adoring Him in my pain? How often did I pray only for healing instead of communicating with Him from my yet unhealed place? How many times had I missed Him in my migraines?

Our small places of weakness are where we can find Him to be strong. Adoration is a beautiful reach from weakness.

FROM PSALM 18:1–3

You are my strength when I have no strength.

On some days I despise my weakness, on others I ignore it, and I often miss You as strong. You are available to me in the moments I resent, casting strength and lifting me out of what I would rather endure.

You change flesh into holiness when I come, weak, and see You as strong.

My weakness is not a reflection of You, but Your strength changes me. I adore You for turning a despised moment into glory with Your strength. I praise You for making strength reach down and come near when I can barely reach back.

You move close with Your strength in my utter weakness. I adore You for who I become when I see You in strength. I adore You for turning my despised weakness into places of encounter.

MY STRENGTH

1 Chronicles 16:11 | Psalm 18:1–3 | Psalm 28:7–8 | Psalm 29:11 | Psalm 46:1 | Psalm 59:16–17 | Psalm 68:35 | Psalm 71:3 | Psalm 73:26 | Psalm 118:14 | Psalm 119:28 | Isaiah 12:2 | Isaiah 40:29–31 | Isaiah 41:10 | 2 Corinthians 1:8–10 | 2 Corinthians 12:9–10 | Philippians 4:13 | Revelation 12:10–11

TINY (BIG) PRAYERS

"God is the strength of my heart" (Ps. 73:26).

"Strengthen me according to Your word" (Ps. 119:28).

"I will strengthen you" (Isa. 41:10).

"I can do all things through Christ who strengthens me" (Phil. 4:13).

DIALOGUE WITH HIM

Identify two or three areas of your life where you feel weak and you despise that weakness. If you can, write them out. Select three or four verses from the list in the "My Strength" section by which to adore. Picture yourself in a moment of weakness even if you aren't currently in it, and adore Him from that place. Let yourself feel His strength penetrating that weakness. Imagine how different your weak areas might feel with the awareness of His strength.

Now prepare.

Ask Him to alert you to the next time you feel weak. (We are often not aware enough to notice when we feel weak. Instead, we react with forced strength.) Prepare with one of those verses by which you will adore at the moment you feel weak. Thank Him for His strength. Ask Him to make that moment different from what you have experienced before.

When the time comes and you walk into that weak moment, adoring Him as your strength, notice what feels different.

4 | HEALER

Jesus said, "Take away the stone."
—JOHN 11:39

IN THE GRIT

Twelve years of infertility taught me that hope is dangerous. Twelve years taught me it is safer not to hope. The potent force of hope, month after month, put me on the razor's edge: waiting, watching. Risking.

Many encouraged me to accept my lot, to settle into what He had given me in a barren womb and a not-yet-healed body. My disagreement with that advice became clear each month when I saw what hope did to me. Hope peeled back layers of the time-roughened exterior. It made me vulnerable. It softened me to Him. Had I chosen to "accept my lot," I would have taken myself away from that razor, that lance into my heart.

Hope isn't safe, but it is healing.

My heart began mending toward Him long before He healed my body. The real story of my healing happened in my heart over the years before that wonderful morning when we discovered that I was carrying a baby. But as I am learning with this healed body, knowing God as healer is a lifetime discovery.

I still ache at baby showers. I cried at mine, feeling the pain from years of sisterhood birth stories that I could not understand. I never questioned His ability to heal, watching the testimonies of His hand in the people around me and reading the testimonies of His hand in His Word. My question was whether the goodness of His healing would ever rest on me. Even after He healed me, the question lingered. Odd, I know, but the question of God's goodness to *me* holds years of layers.

I adore Him as healer, now with my healed body, yet I remain tentative, unable to erase the ache of years. I became vigilant in the waiting room of infertility, watching His goodness fall on others as if it were some spell that skipped over me. I studied their lives against my own, making a case for why the Good Healer might not heal me.

Adoration, now, is a trickle of water against the hardened clay that formed around my heart in the hurting years. He is still healing me on the inside from the pain of hope deferred.

Today I adore Him through one phrase of one story that reveals one aspect of Him. "Jesus said, 'Take away the stone'" (John 11:39–44). He entered into death. He did what no man could do. The boundaries of time and life and existence were His to supersede. He had the stone moved on His way to heal.

I picture His divine ability to shift in a moment, that shift spoken with a human voice from a human body. I adore Him as I picture this healing moment.

And as I adore through this phrase, that stone feels like the wall around my heart. Years of unclean thinking—wrong thinking—permitted a wall around my heart that inhibited my communion with Him. Yet my honest and vulnerable ache did not annoy Him or deter Him from reaching me. Yes, even years after my womb opened, the wall around my heart from that wait and that loss still needs His declaration: "Take away the stone."

As I adore, the trickle of water wets the hardened clay. One part softens. The wall is not yet removed, but the healer proves that it is not impenetrable. I still adore Him as healer, still need to know He heals, even as I wear this healed body.

He reaches our hearts when He delays our bodies. He touches our hearts when He heals our bodies. Our knowledge of Him as a healer may need to accrue over a lifetime. More than instant healing is required to remove these walls of doubt and resistance to the hope that I have formed.

Adoration is the tool He wields — His Word, through my mouth.

Today I heal a little bit more — in my healed body with healing in my heart — as I adore.

AND HERE, IN THE MIDDLE MINUTES, WE ADORE

FROM JOHN 11:39

You heal. You exist as a healer, long before we witness Your healing. And You heal body and soul.

Perhaps harder to heal than my body is my hardened soul. You reached through my broken body to initiate healing there, and I adore You for the healing — the bringing me back to You, back to communion with You, through Your healing hand.

Your hand heals my insides. It removes the stone.

Before they removed the stone to reveal Your resurrected body, You asked them to remove another stone.

Daily, You remove the calcifications around my heart.

You heal me as You reach me. You reach me where no one can see me. You reach the hurt I don't identify. You heal my insides, God, and I adore You.

And You heal in Your time.

MY HEALER

Exodus 15:26 | Psalm 30:2–3 | Psalm 41:3 | Psalm 103:2–4 | Psalm 107:19–21 | Psalm 147:3 | Isaiah 53:5 | Jeremiah 17:14 | Matthew 4:23 | Matthew 9:28–29 | Matthew 10:1 | Matthew 14:14 | Mark 5:25–34 | Luke 13:10–13 | Luke 18:35–43 | John 5:8 (context: John 5:1–15) | John 11:38–44 | Acts 9:33–34 | Acts 10:38 | James 5:14–16 | 1 Peter 2:24

TINY (BIG) PRAYERS

"I am the LORD who heals you" (Ex. 15:26).
"I cried out to You, and You healed me" (Ps. 30:2).
"He heals the brokenhearted" (Ps. 147:3).
"Heal me, O Lord" (Jer. 17:14).

DIALOGUE WITH HIM

Healing is a loaded topic. I don't intend to have us debate about His ability to heal or what it means when He doesn't heal or our faith related to healing. But I do want to invite you to explore God as a healer and, in doing so, make way for a more intimate dialogue with God about how you see Him.

Where have you needed healing and not seen His healing hand? How do you struggle to believe Him as a healer? In that area, choose two or three verses from the list by which to adore. As you adore, ask Him to reveal Himself to you as a healer—on the inside (in my opinion, the harder place for us humans to receive healing). Press pause on asking for the physical manifestation of His healing (allow all the mental traffic that might come as you wait on that ask) and ask Him to heal your heart's understanding of Him as a healer.

For those who journal, this may be an ongoing opportunity to write to Him in your journal, not just a one-time conversation.

5 | BRIDEGROOM

> "I will betroth you to Me forever;
> Yes, I will betroth you to Me in
> righteousness and justice, in loving-
> kindness and mercy; I will betroth
> you to Me in faithfulness, and you
> shall know the LORD."
>
> —HOSEA 2:19–20

IN THE GRIT

Good men get formed, not born. I didn't know this when I walked down the aisle—a slip of a thing in age and size—to marry my man and change my name. A dozen people, at least, must have told us that a person continues to get formed within the context of marriage and not before; however, I settled on fantasy. I scripted an idealistic perspective of our early married years—and of him—that crumbled when two humans got involved. Thus, many of our newly-wed days held strife.

I wanted all the attributes of a godly man in his forties or fifties, with little understanding of what those men walked through in their twenties and thirties to get there. I wanted a hero and a best friend, a man with strong arms to carry me through my weakness and a strong heart to process his. I wanted him to have wisdom beyond his years and the playfulness of youth. And I desperately needed to feel his fierce, unwavering commitment to me, despite my demanding and unrealistic expectations of him.

I verbalized none of this. I wrote none of it in my journal and brought none of these expectations into our premarital counseling. (I left little room for comment or course correction.) Instead, I lived our newlywed days in a malaise of foggy disappointment and disillusionment. At twenty-four, Nate lived a fierce loyalty to me and an unusual commitment to work on the parts of our marriage that disappointed my unrealistic expectations; all the while, I stewed in resentment. I looked past a hundred points in his favor and singled out the few places where he lacked.

"One day you will be grateful for this weakness in him," a friend told me on a morning run as I described my most recent issue with Nate. Those words fell dead for ten years until God resurrected them.

In the interim, I wrestled with unfulfilled longing I couldn't name, the unmet longing that is universal to every human being, married or unmarried.

God made me to know myself, to fully see myself. My craving to have each part of me seen and received came from Him, this God whose "eyes saw my unformed body" (Ps. 139:16 NIV) and who "formed my inward parts" (Ps. 139:13). Thus, all the desire I bring into marriage has its full reception in Him.

Eighteen years later, as I type, Nate astounds me. His gaps, at twenty-four, called forth a reach in him that grew him into more at forty-two than I had imagined he could be. (I write this as a word of hope, because I know from experience that many of you reading these words struggle to hope for your marriage. Ours was a rock-ridden road that only God could redeem.)

However . . . *however*, even the man Nate is at forty-two cannot meet the longing God placed in me, from birth, for a bridegroom. He never will. At best, he can be merely the scent of that for which God intends to fulfill in Himself.

In my twenties, full of unrealistic expectations and fairy-tale dreams, I took my grief to God. After long years of taking my grief to Nate in the form of a list of things to change, I surrendered. I asked God, instead of Nate, to fill me.

Over the *years*, I asked God to fill me.

Desire feels scary, but if brought to Him, He gives context. I brought my unmet desire to the God who calls Himself bridegroom and began to find—through my study of Him as the bridegroom and my adoration of this side of Him—that He could receive the darkest, loneliest, most alienated places of my heart.

This side of God is, perhaps, new to you. All of us—unmarried, married, divorced, widowed—ache for an un-bending, unwavering, unchallenged commitment of love. We ache for an "I will never leave you nor forsake you" in the face of our murkiest thoughts, feelings, and actions. This side of God reaches through the layers and into the ache to respond to the desire we fear.

This God-man is born, not formed. For us.

FROM HOSEA 2:19–20

You are my bridegroom. You take me for Yours, now and for the future and for always. You see the parts of me that I hide, and You betroth them. You covenant me. You don't slink back from my failings as I do, You lean in and You marry. You marry all that I despise and my favorite quirks. You marry all of me, God.

You promise, and You fulfill Your promise, and You exercise the lovingkindness of Yourself in our covenant. I break our covenant, and You fulfill. I am unfaithful, and You remain. I squander, and You love more. I run, and You chase.

The faithfulness that is "us" is You, all You. I adore You for binding Your covenant to my heart, for covenanting me into a loyalty that is not mine, and for making me Yours forever.

You respond to my desire for a forever companion with You. You respond to my desire for You. I adore You, God, and I am responsive and available to meet me with You.

MY BRIDEGROOM

Psalm 45:10–11 | Song of Solomon 4:9–10 | Song of Solomon 7:10 | Hosea 2:16 | Hosea 2:19–20 | Isaiah 54:5 | Isaiah 62:4–5 | Matthew 22:2 (context: Matt. 22:1–14) | Matthew 25:1 (context: Matt. 25:1–13) | Mark 2:19–20 | John 3:29–30 | 2 Corinthians 11:2 | Ephesians 5:25–32 | Revelation 19:7–9 | Revelation 22:17

"I will betroth you to Me forever" (Hos. 2:19).

"Your Maker is your husband" (Isa. 54:5).

"As the bridegroom rejoices over the bride, so shall your God rejoice over you" (Isa. 62:5).

"The Spirit and the bride say, 'Come!'" (Rev. 22:17).

DIALOGUE WITH HIM

Let's get honest with ourselves before Him. Where do you feel the lack of faithful betrothal? And how does it show up in your day-to-day life? (For me, early in our struggling marriage, I wanted deep connection, but didn't know how to get that with Nate; I often felt lonely. Despite his efforts and mine, in our immaturity and lack of self-awareness, we couldn't reach each other. This was my day-to-day lack.)

Whether you are single or married (in a marriage that lacks heart-connection) or widowed (having lost your once-deep connection) or divorced (wondering how to manage the ache of loss), He wants to meet you (me, us) as Bridegroom.

Before you adore, consider whether this aspect of God is new to you. If it is, allow for extra time on the verses in the "My Bridegroom" section and extra time in adoration.

Considering the lack of faithful betrothal and how the ache shows up in your life, choose two to three verses from the list by which to adore. As you adore, ask Him to open your mind to this side of Him. Take note of your resistance (even as you read the verses) and ask Him to help you receive Him despite the resistance you feel.

6 | FATHER

For unto us a Child is born, unto us
a Son is given; and the government
will be upon His shoulder. And His
name will be called Wonderful,
Counselor, Mighty God, Everlasting
Father, Prince of Peace.

—ISAIAH 9:6

IN THE GRIT

Baby books tell the stories of days past, memorializing what we're sure to forget. A wisp of hair, the date of baby's first step, a description of the first time she called you "Mommy."

When our first child is born, we look back in our own baby book. *How much did I weigh? How long was my mom in labor? Did I have hair?* And yet this mile marker is one of many my children who were adopted will pass without a record of their past to help inform their current moments.

In our home, we write the baby books as days progress, filling in the forgotten as memory returns, but leaving inevitable gaps. "Unknown" is the word I write on medical forms for our children who were adopted. Even their birth dates are suspect.

A dear friend's daughter who was adopted is invited to tell her story in an English assignment. *Some stories need a safe audience,* I think. *A haven for a hearing that surely isn't a middle-school lit class.*

But our world barrels on as if orphans are only the stuff of storybooks, living in boxcars and skulking in the corners of the town square, angling for a loaf of bread.

The formerly fatherless, however, live in my home. The pain doesn't lessen with years. But it does heal as it's exposed.

One day we learned a new piece in the story of one of our children. This kind of added information is scarce, and we guard it like a diamond. Yet it feels sharp enough to carve another wound in what was already a thin surface.

The morning after we learned this, I woke to memories of our first days with each of the children we adopted. I could smell the burning trash and motorcycle fuel and hear the goats bleating, all while still in my bedroom. One scene flashed through my mind. It was of one of our children days after we'd brought her into our fold.

Just days after she was ours, we were kicking up African dirt and making small talk on a walk to the market.

"How was life at your orphanage?" I asked awkwardly, reaching for more but not knowing how to move away from "what is your favorite color?"

"Good," she said. One sterile word accompanied by a plastic smile. What else was she to say? Sometimes when there's so much ache, you train yourself to see only "good" — plastic good, empty good.

I can still see her face then — so much fear and pain and past life hiding behind her lifeless expression.

This is fatherlessness. That word—used to describe so many on the earth—can feel so distant from my reality, yet I hold back, not admitting that I live it too.

I felt my fatherlessness on that morning of remembering. My dad coached my sports and paid for my wedding and drove ten hours to watch me run the Marine Corps Marathon—and then he died. But parts of my heart were "good," the plastic and empty kind of good. Untouched by God. Fenced.

I started adoring Him as a Father for her, for them—for our children who know the loss of a father. I adored through their emptiness, feeling their pain in the way that a mama can wear the pain of her child.

Isaiah 9:6 calls Him the "Everlasting Father." The forever Daddy. The "I'm never, ever going to walk out on you" Papa. The stable, always available Father.

I couldn't get that close to Him as Father, calling Him everlasting, picturing Him as the answer to everything she had lost, and not have it infringe on my own story. It wasn't enough for me to adore Him as *their* Father, healing their wounds, being forever available to them.

I needed a God who was this close and would never leave. And yes, I needed Him even before my dad left me fatherless a month after my thirty-second birthday. Even those of us who had near dads, the kind who left the world outside the front door to unpack our hearts in the family room or to kneel by our bedsides at night, still have only a shadow of Him as Father.

So I leaned in a little to what hurt—a pain I'd forgotten until the quiet of that morning. And in my hurt, I leaned into Him. I pictured Him doing what a dad would do as I put His

122

Word in my mouth. "You're an everlasting Father. You never leave. You outlast any pain I might feel. You're always my Dad," I said as I envisioned the rugged eyes of the man Jesus not merely wanting to proselytize me but to see me. To wrap His sturdy frame around all that feels weak in me.

I pictured Him in the nearness of Fatherhood with work-worn hands, earning for my siblings and me, spending for our good. Saying His Word back to Him scooted me a little bit closer to what was true: *I was fatherless, and I needed Him to father me.*

AND HERE, IN THE MIDDLE MINUTES, WE ADORE

USING ISAIAH 9:6

You are my Dad, forever.

Not much lasts long for me. My interests fade, my energy wanes each day, the sun tugging it into hiding as it slips into night. My joy feels temporal and my peace disruptable.

But You, Father.

Your love lasts beyond my capacities. It outlives my insecurities and my energy surges.

Your love outruns me.

You father me through the minutes when I want to climb into Your lap, and You still father me when my flash-pot attention span is on to the next thing. You father me when I seek You, and You father me when I'm afraid of what life in You might mean. You father me when I scoot away from You.

123

I adore You for being my forever father—not merely forever enduring me, but forever fathering me.

I worship You, Father, for tending to the parts of me that I don't realize need a dad. I worship You for whispering with Your life, applied to mine, "I won't leave. I'm here, forever."

Now and on the other side, I will forever need a father. Now and on the other side, You will be Father. I adore You.

MY FATHER

Psalm 68:5 | Psalm 103:13 | Proverbs 3:11–12 | Isaiah 9:6 | Matthew 6:26 | Matthew 18:12–14 | John 14:1–2 | Romans 8:15–16 | James 1:17 | 1 John 3:1

TINY (BIG) PRAYERS

"You received the Spirit of adoption by whom we cry out 'Abba, Father'" (Rom. 8:15).
"Behold what manner of love the Father has bestowed on us, that we should be called children of God!" (1 John 3:1).
"Everlasting Father" (Isa. 9:6).

DIALOGUE WITH HIM

We push through. We become accustomed to functioning with the parts of ourselves that were not fathered, and we neglect the areas of our hearts that live fatherless.

In my life, hyper-productivity is linked to the parts of my heart that disconnect from Him as Father. When I feel good because I've accomplished something and feel foggy or down when I've not, it tells a deeper story. I'm attempting to earn my keep. I want to produce for Him, rather than allow myself the safety of being His daughter who cannot lose her standing.

As you consider Him as Father, ask Him, *What are the areas of my life where I'm living as if I am fatherless?* This isn't a hasty question but one you ask and wait, through the silence, for Him to reveal the answer to. Pay attention.

As He highlights places in you that seem to be living separate from His safe eyes, ask Him for His touch in these places. Ask Him to show Himself to you as Father right within those places.

Take those places and apply one or two of the verses listed in the "My Father" section. Adore from the independent areas of your life and ask Him, as you adore, to show Himself to you as your Dad, right there.

7 | PERSONAL-TO-ME GOD

Lord, all my desire is before You;
and my sighing is not hidden from
You.

—PSALM 38:9

IN THE GRIT

The house sighs, mostly empty. Our Kansas City winter day feels balmy at 55 degrees. All the children play outside, coatless, but one. I know she's inside because I hear her.

She plays chords in the basement, confidently belting out her latest favorite song, like when she had toddler zeal for all things imagined. Except she isn't pretending. Twelve and determined, she fills the pages of her journal with her song lyrics. She studies the techniques of her favorite worship leaders and songwriters. Singing and songwriting are all she wants to do.

Last year, an opportunity opened for her not to only sing but also to participate as an apprentice of sorts, leading worship for her peers. Her Thursday morning piano lessons and voice instruction had angled her in this direction as she buried herself in piles of printed lyrics and chords stacked around her keyboard and on the piano and at her bedside.

But we said a thoughtful no.

Skilled and full of desire, she is passionate about music. God made her to sing, and she comes alive in the doing.

We hedged her in with our careful no. It wasn't time.

The hedge is also mine, at thirty years her senior.

God parents me too.

Last weekend, I drove a luxurious thirty minutes to a speaking engagement. No plane, no packing, no notes for Nate on the counter. I spoke onstage twice, and both times I felt the power of God. The day before this adoption conference, I told Nate, "I've been too busy living life with our children to prepare as much as I want." By my standards, I was underprepared, but prayerful and expectant. And He moved through my scanty notes.

As I drove across town to return to my home, I thought, *He breathed through me today.*

I love to communicate the heart of God. Public speaking turned out to be my favorite (and hardest) class my freshman year. Grizzled and tightfisted with his A's, Mr. Schroom scared me with his erratic rants and one-eyed glares, but the thrill of the class remained. I honed the skill of speaking about uninteresting topics, and it bled into my passions. Years later, standing in front of a basement swollen with sweating Young Life teenagers, I shared the gospel with the same thought that came to me after the adoption conference: "He breathed through me today."

Except this time, a reminder followed that thought: *Not yet. Not now. Not in full.*

I hold many desires that sit in the waiting room. I have dreams for our children, hopes for their restoration, and desires for our home that all seem to have to take a number and then collect dust.

Desire isn't mine to fulfill. But it is mine to carry, to cup within my hands and name. To steward by putting it before Him.

How nuanced. My mind isn't accustomed to catch and release, especially the things that are riveted to my insides.

So I carry my desire to the place of conversation: adoration.

I adore Him through Psalm 38:9: "Lord, all my desire is before You; and my sighing is not hidden from You."

As I say these words back to Him, I realize that I don't believe them in the subtle corners of my thinking. I guard desire as if I assume that if I don't, no one will see it. No one will witness. No one will know. It's all too personal. Too private.

I adore through the pain of holding desire—alone. I read-pray these words and adore Him for being so personal that He even receives my sighs, and I start to see myself as a sharer of desire. Could His desire and mine be commingled? Perhaps desire isn't a dirty word when I put it before Him to witness. To hold. To steward.

Perhaps He is personal enough not only to witness my actions but also to witness my desire behind my actions.

AND HERE, IN THE MIDDLE MINUTES, WE ADORE

USING PSALM 38:9

God, You are more personal to me than I allow my mind to consider.

My desire threatens stretch marks; it feels so large against the constraints of my insides.

But yet I am not responsible for its fulfillment.

You. You, God, You see. And in Your seeing, You relieve me.

Able to carry, but unburdened from fulfilling. Unburdened from parenting my desire, I am a child again at Your invitation.

You watch me. Witness me. You see my desirous sighs. And under Your personal eyes, I become unconstrained.

I adore You, Father, who not only acknowledges desire but sees the ticktock of how it plays on my insides. I adore You for Your beholding. Me. Just as I am—now.

I feel emptied of the unnecessary weight of desire because of You. Free to live and explore and sigh, as You carry and watch and hold.

PERSONAL-TO-ME GOD

Psalm 38:9 | Psalm 20:4 | Psalm 56:8 | Psalm 68:19 | Psalm 139:1, 13, 16–17 | Psalm 145:16 | Matthew 6:8 | Matthew 10:30–31 | Luke 1:25 | John 1:48 | John 4:17–18 | John 11:33

TINY (BIG) PRAYERS

"You formed my inward parts" (Ps. 139:13).
"How precious also are Your thoughts to me" (Ps. 139:17).
"My sighing is not hidden from You" (Ps. 38:9).

What "smaller" things in your life have you kept to yourself, away from Him? What do you have a hard time believing He witnesses with care?

As you adore through the verses in the "Personal-to-Me God" section, pay attention. Pay attention to your heart and your thoughts. What are the places of your life that you don't put before Him? What do you reserve? What don't you bring into your dialogue with God?

After noting them, consider one or maybe two that you could bring into your conversation with God. Ask Him to show you how Psalm 38:9 is related to this area. Ask Him to reveal to your heart and understanding that He sees, He knows.

Consider journaling, or mulling it over on a walk, or talking with a friend about this carefully reserved area of your heart and your protective strategies. As you ask Him to show you Himself as personal, a safe starting place is to acknowledge before Him how you resist this. Repent of this resistance—this self-protective withholding—with the picture in your mind of God as a kind God receiving your repentance (Rom. 2:4).

Ask Him to forgive and cleanse the distance you created, and invite His Spirit to reveal to you how personal He is.

8 | GOD WHO IS MERCIFUL TOWARD THE WEAK ME

He does not delight in the strength of the horse; He takes no pleasure in the legs of a man. The LORD takes pleasure in those who fear Him, in those who hope in His mercy.

—PSALM 147:10–11

IN THE GRIT

The early spring air felt crisp the morning I stepped off my front stoop and walked down our gravel drive for the last time until summer. On the last stretch of a short run, I slipped on a patch of mud and fell, fracturing my ankle. I called Nate in tears. He came, picked me up, put me in the car, and drove back to the house. My feet wouldn't travel that same stretch of driveway again until August.

I also couldn't walk the stairs or carry the little one. My crutches sank into the path through the woods that neighbored our property. No more nature walks. I couldn't stand in the kitchen to cook dinner unless—like a cooking show—someone did all my prep work. No tucking children into bed, no driving, no activities that didn't allow space for a large, hard boot.

The thought of potential weakness makes me suck in my breath as if preparing for what I resist. Weakness challenges my identity.

Who am I as a mother when I cannot rock toddlers to bed or take big girls out for a cup of tea? Who am I as a responsible member of humanity when I can't clean up my trash, cook a meal, or take a shower by myself? These were on the surface, the low-hanging fruit of my mind. I felt the chaos in my home and the unproductive days in bed. I felt uncertainty about my physical capabilities in the future if the break didn't heal properly. Before this, I didn't realize how much my thriving depended on a few variables, things I assumed were untouchables.

I noticed that my peace and even my sense of connectedness to God was contingent upon my strength.

When the house was clean, I felt peace.

When I could smell fresh air and breathe in the everyday murmurs of nature on a morning run or a walk in the woods, I felt fresh and connected to God.

When I could meet our children's needs, I assessed myself as a good mom. I felt good about my motherhood.

The list went on. Each of these things is not bad—tending to a child's needs and having a daily rhythm of outdoor walks or runs and keeping order—and are things I still incorporate into my day now. But what about when I don't have them?

The question that haunts all of us at times is, "What about when the pillars of my day or my life get challenged?"

Two months in a cast revealed my heart to me, as it did God's.

I like myself better when I am strong and productive and on time. I like myself better when I can help myself and help others and feel needed.

And then when I couldn't do those things, I started to see His heart: He likes me when I am weak.

He moves most powerfully when I don't have my strength. He is not impressed by my productivity or my meeting of others' needs or my help. His currency is not my currency, and it took a boot cast, a propped-up ankle, and the same verses I had sung in songs for years but now seeped past my mind into my heart to see His mercy.

I adored God from Psalm 147:10–11 and didn't just acknowledge Him but felt Him run His hands along my cast and look deep into my weak day and take pleasure in me. He liked me when I didn't produce but looked at Him. I learned as I adored. I spoke what didn't feel true when my insides were reeling from all that I couldn't do until I saw the God-man behind those words.

And my hope got whittled to one thing: Him.

I couldn't cook dinner. *God, only Your mercy can gather us around a table.* I couldn't clean or drive to friends' houses or doctors' appointments or dinner dates: *Only Your mercy can cover over what I cannot do.*

I felt His kind eyes toward my weakness as I adored, and I watched Him move in to fix and mend and make something of the minutes when I had nothing to bring.

AND HERE, IN THE MIDDLE MINUTES, WE ADORE

USING PSALM 147:10–11

You are merciful.

You take pleasure in me when I look at You, when I fear You.

*You don't measure my strength, my ability, my
productivity, God. You don't see me as I so often see
me. I can despise me, yet You look at me, and You
find delight in me.*

*I praise You, God, for Your mercy that is not
contingent upon my performance or my self-
sufficient strategies or my wherewithal. I resent my
ill performance, and You lean into me, here. You
don't look away, You look in with mercy.*

*You are generous in mercy to those who look to You.
Even if my look is just a glance. You see my weak
reach, and You give mercy in response. You like me
in my weakness when my eyes rest on You.*

*Your pleasure in me hinges not on my performance
but where I set my eyes. I adore You for this currency
of mercy.*

GOD WHO IS MERCIFUL TOWARD THE WEAK ME

Psalm 5:7 | Psalm 6:2 | Psalm 31:7 | Psalm 31:16 | Psalm
103:11–14 | Psalm 119:76 | Psalm 145:8–9 | Psalm 145:14 |
Psalm 147:10–11 | Lamentations 3:22–23 | Isaiah 54:9–10 |
Romans 5:6–8 | 1 Corinthians 1:26–27 | 2 Corinthians 12:9
| 1 Timothy 1:16 | Hebrews 4:15–16

TINY (BIG) PRAYERS

"My strength is made perfect in weakness" (2 Cor. 12:9).
"[He is] slow to anger and great in mercy" (Ps. 145:8).
"He knows our frame" (Ps. 103:14).

Psalm 145:14 reads, "The Lord upholds all who fall, and raises up all who are bowed down." We have two stances to consider in this psalm. Think about the last time you fell in some way, whether it be in sin or in weakness. How did you see Him in that moment? (Take time to sit with this question and allow yourself to perceive your response to your sin and failings before God.)

To bow down in true repentance requires us to move past shame and into the confidence of how He responds to His people in their sin. Shame keeps us defending ourselves and working toward behavior modification. Repentance brings us to our knees, desperate for what He can give: mercy. Now consider the last time you responded to your sin with a genuine repentance, your heart bowing before Him.

Both of these questions may leave you realizing you've neither trusted Him to respond to your sin and failure with an arm that upholds nor felt safe before His eyes to allow yourself to bow in repentance, trusting that He will raise you.

From this place of realization—whatever you have noted about your heart's posture from this time—adore Him as the God who is merciful, upholds you when you fall, and lifts you when you come to Him in your failure. Use the verses in this section to adore this side of God that is unfamiliar.

9 | GOD WHO FIGHTS FOR ME

He shall send from heaven and save me; He reproaches the one who would swallow me up.

—PSALM 57:3

IN THE GRIT

Time slowed on this night. The spring breeze through the half-open window carried the still chilly air of winter warming in the day's sun. Spring's hope was palpable. Robins and blue jays chattered in the bushes that line our eating nook. The children talked over one another, each with something more important to share than the last, the ease and joy of family overruling manners this night. Virginia the extrovert squealed. Her countenance is the family mirror.

Nate and I started talking about old music. He gave a five-minute lesson to eager listeners on music from before our time—the Beach Boys and Van Morrison, Buddy Holly and the Supremes—which quickly morphed into a sing-along. Nate and I danced around the kitchen to songs we sang as kids, singing into our spoons and using the table and the stools and kitchen island as our stage, with four-year-old Bo dancing between us. The big kids shouted, "More!" after every song, enthralled and not at all embarrassed by the spectacle their parents made of themselves. The birds were the only other witnesses to this performance.

We were twenty-three again, unaware of bedtimes or kitchen cleanup responsibilities or the mess that deep-belly-laughing fun can make.

Our kids still talk about that night.

An hour later, as I rocked Virginia before bedtime, the fear that comes after the best moments in life crouched at the door. I put her to bed, but my fear remained.

Crazy fear, maybe? But familiar.

Instead of relishing the glint Lily had in her eyes when she shouted, "More," and the reprieve deep belly laughter gives to hearts that hurt, and the reminder that Nate and I can clear a dance floor, I feared when the next tragedy would strike, the destruction lurking in the shadows.

I fell asleep aware, this time, of fear's habit to steal.

The next morning, I remembered my fears more than the candles flickering in the spring breeze across the kitchen table or Virginia shouting, "Mommy! Daddy!" as we danced. Self-awareness helped me to identify the pattern, but self-awareness was not enough to get me out of it.

Before I could attach legitimacy to any one of the slinky fears, I opened my Bible to Psalm 57:3 — the adoration verse I had assigned, a month earlier, to this day.

Instead of evading the fear, I considered it. *What if?*

It's the worst strategy for defusing fear, yet His Word has power over even the worst strategies.

I applied His promise from Psalm 57:3 to "save me" to every fear I felt, wanting to be sure that He had a response to what might steal.

It held ground. I didn't feel it at first because of how

strongly I felt my fear. But as I adored Him, the one who fights for me, something within me settled a little bit deeper into the understanding that He would fight for me should any of these fears come true.

If we had a tonic that could dispel fear with one chug, no one would turn it down, but the fight against fear is a lifetime commitment to growth in communing with God. Trust is birthed and grows as we face our fears and turn to Him. This morning's adoration wasn't that tonic. Adoration isn't a solution; it's a pathway to communion and conversation.

As I adored, I grew in trust. Although the fear has crouched at my door again, it has become less potent.

AND HERE, IN THE MIDDLE MINUTES, WE ADORE

FROM PSALM 57:3

You save me. You fight for me. You defend me against my enemies.

Most days my enemy is the fear within me—more significant than my circumstances, more significant than whatever happens. As I run to You, fear dissipates. Simply by falling into Your arms, the weight of fear lifts. You fight for me as You hold me, God.

You save me from my fear. You don't scold or chastise me for coming to You in need of saving. You "reproach the one who would swallow me up." My fear.

I adore You, God, for fighting for me so that I don't have to fight for me. I come to You, and You fight. You take my weakness, and You turn it into Your battle.

I adore You, my defender.

GOD WHO FIGHTS FOR ME

Exodus 15:2–3 | Deuteronomy 3:22 | Deuteronomy 20:4 | 2 Samuel 22:3 | Psalm 3:3 | Psalm 5:11 | Psalm 9:4 | Psalm 20:1–2 | Psalm 57:3 | Psalm 59:1–2 | Psalm 62:2 | Psalm 71:24 | Psalm 72:12–14 | Psalm 108:13 | Psalm 118:6 | Psalm 140:7 | Isaiah 35:3–4 | Romans 8:34–37

TINY (BIG) PRAYERS

"Your God is He who goes with you, to fight for you" (Deut. 20:4).

"Deliver me" (Ps. 59:1).

"Through God we will do valiantly" (Ps. 108:13).

"The Lord is on my side; I will not fear" (Ps. 118:6).

DIALOGUE WITH HIM

Though there are many ways to consider God as the one who fights for us, let's sit for a minute in the notion that fear wants to steal what God gives. Fear can be a barrier to communion, or our communion can dispel our fear.

When was your glorious night, the one that fear chased? Perhaps it wasn't a night but an opportunity or a gift. Something too good to be true. How have you seen fear or doubt lurk at the doorway after God gives you a gift? How did you respond when it did?

Let's prepare. Adore God using one or two of the verses in the "God Who Fights for Me" section as you consider the last time fear sought to chase away God's gift. Let Him enter that moment even though it has passed. Invite His Spirit to give you another way to see fear, as you adore.

And then choose one of the verses to have available to adore with the next time fear chases your wondrous moment.

10 | GOD WHOSE THOUGHTS ARE HIGHER THAN MINE

And do not be conformed to this world,
but be transformed by the renewing of your
mind, that you may prove what is that good
and acceptable and perfect will of God.

—ROMANS 12:2

IN THE GRIT

"Should" got sneaky, and it got sophisticated.

A cursory examination of my thought-life revealed "should" as a marker, an indicator that duty drove me harder than connectedness to the Father. I paid attention, flagging "should" every time it surfaced in my thoughts, pausing to reflect rather than respond.

So "should" got smarter. It masked itself in other phraseology, hiding within my thinking again.

The morning broke without notice on Tuesday. My thoughts drummed like a parade through the quiet. *I need to contact my friend, who is sick* morphed into *I'm not a faithful friend*. How many times had I forgotten to call her? And then to a scalding, *Why can't I remember these things?*

Following these thoughts came a similar, progressive litany about our children and then my writing. No area of my life felt unscathed from the morphing "should." According to my thoughts, with only a fifth of the day lived awake, I had failed in friendship, lacked in motherhood, and shouldn't call myself a writer.

I hadn't poured my morning tea yet but felt a kind of terrible that no amount of caffeine could relieve.

I'd gotten used to terrible. Terrible was normal. Safe, even, in the way an orphaned child finds street life safer than a bed and a home and a mom and dad. They choose what they know until choosing isn't a conscious act anymore.

This morning was choiceless. Not all that different from the one before it or the one that would follow it. I caged myself in the safety of all the morphed shoulds because the alternative felt far too unfamiliar.

Until I considered adoration.

Even if it was merely a rote habit, I could adore alongside entertaining all the thoughts of what I should do and what I wasn't; we don't perceive His Word as intercepting our negative thought swirl until we let it.

I gave permission, even though within minutes I would try to take it back. In so doing came this hint of a question: What if He doesn't think these things about me?

Which led to another thought: Maybe I'm not meant to host these thoughts.

And only a tinge of another: I think I am stuck here.

Then, just as quickly as it came, one hapless morning turned.

I adored Him through Romans 12:2, arguing as I adored.

Doesn't being conformed to this world have to do with how I spend my money and where I spend my time and what

I say with my mouth? I asked Him, like a schoolgirl, but reading the answer in front of me.

I flitted to "I adore You, God, for making my mind new. I praise You for working transformation on my insides, this terrible, normal morning."

My words rolled out the red carpet for my heart. His Words rolled out the red carpet for me to inch toward a new place. I didn't want these thoughts to drive me anymore, and His Word whispered freedom from them.

One step on one normal morning makes it easier to take another step the next day. And another the following day. Freedom isn't elusive anymore.

AND HERE, IN THE MIDDLE MINUTES, WE ADORE
USING ROMANS 12:2

God, Your thoughts are higher than mine.

Your will and mine are not the same.

What?!

That cannot be. Except You tell me otherwise when You suggest transformation. I adore You, Father, who renews my mind.

You transform me with Your thoughts about me, thoughts higher than my own.

You give my mind new life with the way You see and think and feel.

You release me from the constraints that my mind erects. Freedom is within my reach. I adore You for freeing me to think like You, to see like You, to own Your thoughts and soon call them mine.

I adore You for the freedom of Your thinking, Your seeing, Your perceiving.

Thank You for giving Yourself to me, You in my mind.

GOD WHOSE THOUGHTS ARE HIGHER THAN MINE

1 Samuel 16:7 | Psalm 89:5–6 | Psalm 119:18 | Psalm 139:1–4 | Psalm 139:17 | Proverbs 21:2 | Isaiah 40:28 | Isaiah 55:8–9 | John 16:12–14 | Romans 11:33–34 | Romans 12:2 | Romans 8:26 | 1 Corinthians 1:25, 27–29 | 1 Corinthians 2:9–11, 14–16 | 1 Corinthians 13:12 | Philippians 4:6–7

TINY (BIG) PRAYERS

"Renew my mind" (Rom. 12:2).
"'The LORD does not see as man sees'" (1 Sam. 16:7).
"Open my eyes, that I may see" (Ps. 119:18).

DIALOGUE WITH HIM

It's time to check the oil. Many times, we take a nebulous assessment of our relationship with God using fuzzy metrics—how we feel about Him, how we think He thinks about us, our performance.

Today let's start with our minds, though not to determine good or bad, naughty or nice. Let's peek into our thoughts and examine how they align with His. Take a notepad with you and write down the thoughts you often dismiss. The best time for this is the downtime when those thoughts surface. As you fold laundry or wait in the car line at school or ride the train into the city, where does your mind wander? What is taking up space in your head?

(A hint: if you're like me, you will find some murky intruders.)

Attentiveness to our thoughts is the beginning of the renewal of our minds. After you write your thoughts in your notebook, consider one that frequents your head that you know is not His. Dig into His Word to find what is true and adore this side of Him. Commit to it for the week ahead or the month ahead. Some of you, like me, may need a year lingering on the truth that His Word opposes how your mind deceives you.

11 | GOD WHO WORE SKIN

Therefore, when Jesus saw her weeping,
and the Jews who came with her weeping,
He groaned in the spirit and was troubled.

—JOHN 11:33

IN THE GRIT

I ended my road run on the beach the morning after we arrived. Up the boardwalk stairs, I could smell the salt of the ocean before I saw it.

Each summer, the year between beach trips created anticipation in me for that first look at the ocean. The ocean didn't change, but I did, and this year it was different.

I forgot as I crested the top of the boardwalk stairs that the previous year at the beach was one of the last times I saw Dad. My dad, the one who indoctrinated me into loving the ocean, made me love claylike sand between my fingers and against my skin, and the mystery of a world that hid beneath the tides. I loved this place because he loved it.

Sometimes, after a long day of building cities in the sand, I'd misidentify an ocean scent for the smell of his salty skin wrapped around my little-girl sunburn. The sand mingled with his freckled body, and I wondered if he wore sand all year long. I didn't know the ocean apart from my daddy.

Until that summer.

Grief caught me by surprise. My memory of my dad surrounded me at the beach. I strangely expected to see him on the other side of the boardwalk. But I was alone, without him.

Is this what they felt the morning after He died or during the days after He ascended? Could they still smell the sweat of His experience against the desert's receiving of Him? Did they picture the look in His eye when they first met Him or the dirt of Gethsemane? Was their last image one of His bearing up under the weight of wood and accusations?

I look at the early church, relentless in love, and wonder what memory did for their devotion.

They saw His eyes.

God wept tears, to them. His calloused fingers brushed their skin. Their *feet.*

They walked with God, and we live our days wondering if the Word, pregnant with promise, could be real to us.

How would I live if I had seen Him smile at me or heard Him laugh at one of my quirks? How would I walk with Him now if I had smelled sweat?

Adoration takes me from where I am, in this twenty-first-century life, to who He was then, and who He is for me now.

Adoration enables me to smell His skin.

The Jesus they remembered lives inside of me. And when I make Him into a principle, a lesson to be extracted, I lose the power of the person I was meant to encounter through His Word.

I sometimes adore God by asking Him to make those

moments in His Word alive to me. I want to step into the gospels and see more than a platitude to apply to my life. I want to look at the lines on His face. I want to smell His skin. I want to adore the person of Jesus.

At dinner, Nate asked the children, "What's your favorite thing that happened in the Bible?" One told about that man who died and Jesus came a few days later to raise him from the dead. Another described Him riding on a donkey. Instead of listening coldly, remotely—thinking of the pile of dishes in the sink and the six things I had to do before I could sleep that night—I fought tears as they described their little-girl versions of the big God, the same God I'd adored days earlier. Adoration moved my insides. They were talking about the Jesus I know.

Just like at the beach, expecting my dad to be around the corner. The scent of His memory hung that thick.

Adoration scoots me next to Him.

AND HERE, IN THE MIDDLE MINUTES, WE ADORE

FROM JOHN 11:1–44

You wore skin for me.

It was that Mary. The one You said who found the "one thing that was needed," now stirred Your spirit again. Did You weep because she wept? She spoke the same words as her sister, in response to this pain and Your delay, yet it was to her that You wept.

What does this say about You, God?

You made Yourself into flesh which could be moved by flesh. You loved. Not cold or distant but stirred by the ones You formed and inside the skin they wore. I adore You, God. You didn't merely put on my frame but allowed Yourself to be moved by my heart cries.

Your Son wept my tears. The God who put on man and lived man's pain made ethereal love real, tangible. O God, who knows me, Your life bent downward so that I would know You on my insides.

You put on skin for me.

You didn't just teach me, You loved me by living in me and then letting me live and breathe You.

You remembered her extravagant love. You, O God, made Yourself to be the one who received from those You made. What kind of love is this?

You knew her not only from creating her but from receiving her offering. You loved her, and her loss made You weep.

I love how You love.

Your wet tears fell on dusty desert roads. Holiness spilled out onto the earth You spoke into existence. Just as You received her, Your earth received a symbol of the humanity You wore in that time when love broke through flesh. The sounds of Your heart, borne outward as You wept, were heard by broken people. You let broken people witness Your body's manifestation of love, broken for them.

I adore You—God made flesh but not compromised.

Your end on the earth made a new beginning for them, for all of them who witnessed. And for me, if I allow myself to hear the words You spoke then, deep in my spirit now.

"Lazarus, come forth!" His end revealed Your power. His death, Your inbreaking.

You confound me, and You scooted near enough then, and still, now, for me to smell the mystery wrapped up in Your skin.

GOD WHO WORE SKIN

Exodus 3:14 | Matthew 1:23 | Mark 6:3 | Luke 2:7 | Luke 2:40 | Luke 2:51–52 | John 1:14 | John 8:58 | John 11:1–44 | John 15:3 | John 15:15b | Romans 3:23–24 | Galatians 4:4 | Philippians 2:5–8 | Colossians 2:9 | 1 Timothy 3:16 | Hebrews 1:1–4 | Hebrews 2:9–10 | 1 Peter 2:4 | 1 John 1:1–2

TINY (BIG) PRAYERS

"You came in the likeness of man for me" (Phil. 2:7).
"You dwelt among us" (John 1:14).
"But we see Jesus, who was made low" (Heb. 2:9).

DIALOGUE WITH HIM

Use John 11:1–44 or another passage from the gospels that depicts Jesus and insert yourself into the account.

What do you see of Him? How does your heart respond to God in the flesh? Take some time to write or pray through how you respond to Jesus' nearness as demonstrated in His Word (and with you in the picture). Permit yourself to feel the impact of God in the flesh—discomfort, distance, cold-heartedness, and all.

Hint: to embrace the nearness of God, we need to stay long enough to note the discomfort we experience when we stay there and talk to God about it.

Use this exercise as your starting point. What parts of His character and His nature, being near you, feel outside of your understanding or comfort level?

Then pray.

Ask Him to make His Word alive to you. (Psalm 119:25 says, "Revive me according to Your word." I pray this prayer often. I need His Word to do this in me.) Spend a few days, or longer, in the gospels and ask Him to reveal new sides of Himself to you in the person of Jesus and His nearness to you. Adore what you see and expect to have new understanding as you do. Ephesians 1:18 says, "The eyes of your understanding being enlightened." Ask for it. This is another prayer to pray as you engage with His Word in this way. Then, if you like to record, write it out.

12 | POWERFUL GOD

In my distress I called upon the LORD, and
cried out to my God; He heard my voice from
His temple, and my cry came before Him,
even to His ears. . . . He sent from above, He
took me. He drew me out of many waters.

—PSALM 18:6, 16

IN THE GRIT

One moment's pain—one circumstance's pain—is not often independent. The date that got canceled takes on hues
of prior relationships that ended. The friendship that went
sour surfaced the sting of two others before it. The marriage
fight showed her using her mother's words, and him his father's. We are a storied people; we bring past stories into our
current moments.

I know I do.

Trauma has a way of distilling into a single moment.

I was driving two of my girls to their drama class before
meeting an out-of-town friend for dinner, preoccupied with
the clock yet present enough to answer a call from my mom.

"The doctor told her to prepare, because it looks like
she has cancer." She spoke of my sister.

For the second time in my life, a diagnosis arrested my normal and a moment became life changing.

In the weeks that followed this news, life couldn't stop for me, but my heart did. My dad had died of cancer nine years earlier. I'd lost a dear friend and also a mentor to cancer within the three years before this phone call. I could recite "O Death, where is your sting?" from 1 Corinthians 15:55 up and down the stairs and on a morning run, but I felt stung. And the sting lingered. I felt a decade younger, facing my dad's diagnosis all over again, but without the ten years of maturing in between. My mind spun with the potentialities, ones I once lived.

"Sara, adore," Nate said after hearing me process that the history I brought into this moment made it especially electric and, thus, debilitating. "This is what we do."

So I did. I brought into my conversation with God a history of diagnoses and doctor's appointments and fear confirmed by test results. I didn't posture. I came angry, with questions I'd buried when we lowered my dad into the ground, but that resurfaced. I knew God could handle me.

With the layers of subconscious posturing peeled away— in the way that raw pain can often gift us—I approached His Word.

After Nate and I spent an hour one afternoon in our friend-and-counselor's office, talking through the history I brought into my situation, I realized that I needed a person to receive the deeper questions of my heart.

The questions I held:

- Is He powerless against sickness and loss?
- Is He good to *me*?
- Is He dispassionate?

I didn't identify two of these three before this diagnosis; I had carried them inside, undetected.

In identifying them with our counselor friend, the pain came uncorked. I moved from numb to deeply aching, the sadness coming over me in waves. I'd worked hard to silence the questions, but now that I had identified them, all the feeling underneath them gave way. I asked God for a psalm—something, anything in His Word that could anchor me in this uncertainty. Psalm 18 came to mind. I spent the following six months working my way through the words.

I adored as I read words I didn't believe. I wouldn't have known I didn't believe them before I permitted the questions. I learned as I adored that the questions are not dangerous if I unfurl them before Him.

Adoration enabled me to say what my mind and heart could not believe, from a place of such vulnerability that His Word washed me. I didn't posture or pretend. I came broken and angry and sad to His Word. I told Him I didn't believe phrases that said He is "my strength," "my shield," "my stronghold," and I pleaded with Him to meet me in my unbelief. I cried onto the pages of my Bible.

Once I uncovered the questions I had worked so hard to stifle, I could not sit in them without asking Him to be near. Numbness felt easier than facing them, but a few brushes with His nearness and His whispers to me as I read, prayed, cried, and adored made numbness less appealing. I wanted an encounter with God that would enable me to face the next diagnosis or the subsequent loss with a personal sense that He had the power to carry me. To heal my doubtful insides. To breathe life into the darkened corners of my thinking.

As I adored Him through Psalm 18, I discovered that the ache over my sister's diagnosis had less to do with the implications on her life and more to do with the questions of God I carried into this circumstance. And I did not need answers; I needed to acknowledge the questions before the God who had a response in Himself. He is powerful to heal our pain, even while we wait on our circumstances.

The well-worn pages of Psalm 18 in my Bible now are a part of my history. I wrote out each of the action verbs as I adored, saying them back to Him and to my weak and questioning heart: *He heard, He flew, He made the darkness His canopy, He sent, He took, He drew, He delivered.*

This chapter grew into the tale of a powerful God who is passionate toward my pain and good when I face loss. Adoration—when I came vulnerable and honest—opened my eyes to see Him. It brought Him into the numbness so that He could uncover what lay beneath it and speak to those pain-filled questions. His answers weren't circumstantial shifts; they were about His person. He knew I needed more than a quick answer to my prayer. I needed a voice speaking into the dark inside of me.

AND HERE, IN THE MIDDLE MINUTES, WE ADORE

FROM PSALM 18:6, 16

You hear.

You send.

You take.

You draw me.

I fear You will be dispassionate, inactive, and
passive to my pain and my heart. But Your Word
tells me You are nearer than I thought. My ache
fuels You. You see me, God.

You advocate.

You save.

You deliver me.

I adore You that when I feel numb and distant,
You have not relented in Your activity toward me. I
praise You that when I go cold on the inside, You are
fighting for my heart. Your power moves through me,
God, if I let it in.

You move me with You.

Then the world around me looks different. I see possibilities
when I look at You. When I read of Your power, I hope.
There is light in what feels dark when I let You in.

I adore You, powerful God, powerfully moving to
save me, to deliver me from myself, to rescue my
heart unto greater connectedness to You.

POWERFUL GOD

Psalm 62:11 | Psalm 66:5–7 | Psalm 105:2 | Psalm 147:4–5 |
Proverbs 30:4 | Isaiah 9:6 | Isaiah 40:21–31 | Jeremiah 32:17
| Daniel 4:35 | Matthew 19:26 | Luke 4:40 | John 19:10–11
| Romans 1:20 | 1 Corinthians 6:14 | Ephesians 1:17–21 |
Ephesians 3:20 | Colossians 1:16–17 | Hebrews 1:3a | Reve-
lation 1:8 | Revelation 19:6

"He is awesome in His doing toward the sons of men" (Ps. 66:5).

"To Him who is able to do exceedingly abundantly above all that we ask or think" (Eph. 3:20).

"Great is our Lord, and mighty in power" (Ps. 147:5).

DIALOGUE WITH HIM

As you read, did you identify a buried question you have about God related to His power in your life? If so, bring that before Him and choose a psalm that speaks to that question. Give yourself time in that psalm. Allow space for other questions to surface toward Him. Note each one with the intention of bringing them to Him as you adore.

Adoration can feel rote if we paste His Words over our pain without talking to Him about it. Permit yourself to speak with God about your pain, as unfamiliar as it may feel. I lived in Psalm 18 for half of a year. Questioning, then receiving, then questioning (and sometimes in anger), then receiving.

If your questions about God and His power in your life don't surface, pay attention in the days ahead and note whether you are responding to a situation with a weightiness that implies deeper questions about Him. Allow yourself to unearth those questions and bring them to Him and to His Word.

13 | GOD, CLOSER THAN MY SKIN

Where can I go from Your Spirit? Or where
can I flee from Your presence? If I ascend into
heaven, You are there; if I make my bed in
hell, behold, You are there. If I take the wings
of the morning, and dwell in the uttermost
parts of the sea, even there Your hand shall
lead me, and Your right hand shall hold me.

—PSALM 139:7–10

IN THE GRIT

Sometimes grief is a gentleman, waiting until we have time
to think and feel before entering the rooms of our interior
lives. Other times grief ignores all the cues, and you weep
over your salad at dinner while celebrating a friend's birthday, or tuck away into a bathroom stall at a concert and cry.

The grief related to my dad's death waited. He died three
months after we brought our first two children home from
Ethiopia, and a year and a half later, we were on a plane to
Uganda to adopt our second two. I allowed little room for
grief, and grief respected my limits. In the backdrop of my
mind, I believed that a bout or two with grief meant that I
had traveled all I needed to in losing my dad. I was wrong.

After child number five came into our family, the grief over losing my dad erupted in full force. Sadness seeped into friendships and motherhood and dinner conversations. I missed more than the father he was when he died; I missed him *now*. The sting of fatherlessness left me floundering. I felt his absence in so many areas of my life.

What do you do about a person you cannot bring back? How do you face unrequited love for a dad when fathers are intended to be stabilizers?

I did what I knew to do, even though I didn't want to. Through my adoration, I invited God to be near. The loss of my dad made me feel miles away from God. My proxy left, and I forgot for whom he was proxying.

Adoration felt out of place against my grief. Mistimed. I wanted to sit in my loss, not because I had a desire to wallow but because any activity took work.

Except adoration, which didn't require me to move. It asked that I invite Him to where I am and let Him lift me.

Psalm 139 is my safe place to start adoring.

He felt far. I adored Him as near, not betraying my feelings but acknowledging (to Him who made me) that I didn't feel what I said.

He felt distant and removed from my ache. I adored Him as the one who didn't shrink from even my darkest, hellish places of thought and heart.

Over days and weeks, I started to see through my pain, not around it. My coping before my adoring was to circumvent the pain. To do what helped me forget it. Adoration relieved me from elaborate efforts to escape.

And it didn't require the kind of hard work that one in grieving cannot muster, but instead, it needed a hand on the latch of the gate, opening the door so that He could come in.

The more I adored with my hand on the latch of the gate, the more I believed what His Word said about Him. He was not holding my hand in my grief. His hand wasn't on my back. He was closer than my skin, healing me as He came nearer than I could imagine.

AND HERE, IN THE MIDDLE MINUTES, WE ADORE
FROM PSALM 139:7–12

You are nearer than my skin, even when I don't think I need You to be near.

I'm running, and You hold me.

I slip into darkness through the cracks formed by life's pain, and You are not hindered by where I go. You are near, even there.

Your presence surrounds me. I cannot run from what encompasses me, and I cannot make it go away. My escape does not shake Your nearness. I run, and I find You.

You are there, nearer than my skin.

I adore You for chasing me to the ends of the earth and the ends of my story and the ends of my pain. You don't chase me to coach me back into a normal place. You chase me to show Your face to me. You come after me, God, and make Yourself near in every minute of my life.

I adore You, God who is closer than my skin.

Psalm 16:8 | Psalm 34:18 | Psalm 46:1 | Psalm 119:151 |
Psalm 139:7–12 | Psalm 145:18 | Isaiah 50:8 | Isaiah 55:6
| John 14:16–17 | John 15:4 | John 16:7 | John 17:26 | Acts
17:27–28 | Romans 8:35 | Ephesians 2:13 | Hebrews 10:19–
20 | James 4:8a | 1 John 4:13

TINY (BIG) PRAYERS

"Where can I go from Your Spirit?" (Ps. 139:7).
"He dwells with you and will be in you" (John 14:17).
"Abide in Me, and I in you" (John 15:4).
"Draw near to God and He will draw near to you"
(James 4:8).

DIALOGUE WITH HIM

Consider one neutral moment from this last week, something in your life that happens every week. By neutral, I
mean one moment that doesn't carry a lot of emotion but is
one of those things in life you need to do. Examples might
be attending your son's soccer game or going grocery shopping or bringing dinner to your parents' home or participat-
ing in a weekly staff meeting.

As you review this moment, have you seen Him (in the
past) intersect that? Have you felt compelled to talk to Him
about it? Has He interrupted your thinking at that moment
with a verse or a thought from Him? If so, narrate that back
to yourself: How did He come? What did He do to interrupt
that moment?

If not, consider Psalm 139:7–10 in light of that weekly
moment and ask Him for His presence there. Adore and ask.
Ask Him to surprise you with His thoughts and His Word.

Consider bringing a notecard or some remembrance of this verse into that moment when it happens next and adore Him for a few minutes. Ask Him to intersect the normal with Himself and show you how near He is when you least expect it.

14 | GOOD-TO-ME GOD

The LORD preserves the simple; I was brought low, and He saved me. Return to your rest, O my soul, for the LORD has dealt bountifully with you. For You have delivered my soul from death, my eyes from tears, and my feet from falling.

—PSALM 116:6–8

IN THE GRIT

When my sister was diagnosed with cancer, I couldn't think. Fog hung over my mind and my thoughts. I didn't feel; I went numb, possibility swirling around my head, doused with fear. I served dinner and drove my kids to appointments, but I lived in a haze.

And then I recognized the breach in my conversation with God.

After her diagnosis, I started to approach Him like my college history professor, who was managing a class of three hundred. I was the student turning in tests. We had nothing to discuss. I was responsible for learning the material; He was the one giving a grade.

This is not my usual mode of relating to God, but in

certain circumstances, I revert to this. I tense my shoulders, "wait it out," and release a sigh when the circumstance seems to pass.

Until a circumstance like this infringes on my thinking again, weeks, months, or even years later.

After my sister's cancer diagnosis, I chose to acknowledge and revisit my deepest question of God, the one that shadows my life intermittently: Is God good to *me*? But I didn't know that this was the question shadowing me, again, until I adored through the fog.

I opened my Bible to Psalm 116:6–8. Those words seemed stark against my insides, which felt murky.

> The LORD preserves the simple;
> I was brought low, and He saved me.
> Return to your rest, O my soul,
> For the LORD has dealt bountifully with you.
> For You have delivered my soul from death,
> My eyes from tears,
> And my feet from falling.
>
> —PSALM 116:6-8

At that moment, I was brought low, separated from His goodness, bare and independent. (The psalmists show us that no emotions are off-limits to God.) I came to Him, identifying the feelings underneath the fog (because fog masks from us not only Him but also ourselves), and told my weak soul what was true of Him: *You deal bountifully with me. You deliver my soul from death. You deliver my feet from falling.*

I disrobed myself of pretense before Him and learned

that my Sunday-school answers kept me from the honesty I needed to grow in intimacy with Him.

Most of the healing came through my experiencing His receiving me in all of my doubt and fear and anger as I adored.

My fog lifted months before my sister was cancer free, a sign of a genuine internal shift.

This is adoration. I bring all of me (as much as I can access from within my fog) to all of Him in His Word, and I let His Spirit reach through that fog to my insides and tell me what's true.

AND HERE, IN THE MIDDLE MINUTES, WE ADORE

FROM PSALM 116:6–8

You are good to me.

When life brings me low, You save me. You deal bountifully with me. You revive me.

When the fog of circumstances hangs threatening and heavy over my life, You break through the fog to reach my soul with Your goodness.

I adore You, God. You are good to me.

You come in my tears, in the foreboding of death, in the storm, and You give me bounty. You give me Yourself. Your goodness supersedes the circumstantial ache. I adore You for Your goodness, ever always available to me.

My feet stumble and I fall, and You save. You are good to me when I cannot carry myself. In my weakness, You are good.

I adore You, God who is better than my circumstances, good in every one.

GOOD-TO-ME GOD

Psalm 13:6 | Psalm 21:6 | Psalm 23:6 | Psalm 27:13 | Psalm 31:19 | Psalm 34:8 | Psalm 36:7–8 | Psalm 37:18 | Psalm 65:11 | Psalm 84:11 | Psalm 103:1–5 | Psalm 115:14–15 | Psalm 116:7 | Psalm 119:68 | Psalm 145:9 | John 1:16 | Romans 8:28 | Romans 8:32 | Ephesians 2:7 | Philippians 1:6 | James 1:17

TINY (BIG) PRAYERS

"No good thing will He withhold" (Ps. 84:11).
"The LORD has dealt bountifully with you" (Ps. 116:7).
"All things work together for good to those who love God" (Rom. 8:28).
"He who has begun a good work in you will complete it" (Phil. 1:6).

DIALOGUE WITH HIM

God doesn't coach us out of our pain, He holds us in it.

Most of us imagine that He's irritated and impatient, wishing that we could be through this and over that. What a lie! God asks us to come like the little children in Matthew 18:2–5 because it is small children who find the comfort of being in His lap, resting against His chest, being held and known and seen.

Adoration asks me to come to Him like that child.

Consider the areas of your life where you feel a fog or a time in your life when that fog was palpable. Unpack this in your mind. Underneath that fog, was there a question of

God's goodness to you? If not this question, then what was the question?

Adoration enables an experience with God now as well as a healing from past experiences when we struggled to see His hand. Allow yourself to consider that fog or that time when He felt elusive and distant and hardened to your pain. Choose two or three verses from the "Good-to-Me God" section and bring your whole self—your childlike self, with all its questions and fears—to adore from that place.

15 | TENDER GOD, GENTLE WITH ME

"I have compassion on the multitude, because they have now continued with Me three days and have nothing to eat. And I do not want to send them away hungry, lest they faint on the way."

—MATTHEW 15:32

IN THE GRIT

Seven humans were packed into a rusting Suburban for a five-week road trip that felt long just a few hours after we turned out of our driveway. I had spent weeks planning meals and outfits and overnight stops and buying car tchotchkes that might make the stretch across the Midwest feel a bit more memorable for fidgety little ones. But I could plan only so much; seven humans meant seven times the opportunity for plans to go astray.

I'd learned when I was fifteen and my dad incurred a back injury that left our family one man down for the rest of his life that a day can feel a bit safer when you have a plan. Though safety is rarely, if ever, anyone's highest goal, many of us bow to it after facing a threat to it.

I was subservient to a desire to have everything go as

planned, but wedged tightly in a car with six of my people who are fallible.

Two weeks in, I saw that God had invited me to a new and tender conversation with Him on this trip—one where I was alive and His eye was on me—and yet I continued to approach it as if it were a board meeting. We left Colonial Williamsburg and headed for the beach with a plan to arrive before the babe's bedtime. An hour later, and after one stop we'd made between the hotel and our destination, Nate got a phone call. Apparently, in his effort to fit each child's duffle into the back and still have room for the Pack'n Play, he'd left his brief bag, with laptop, resting against the hotel's exterior.

We turned around and I grumbled inside, wondering if God was finally siding with my judgment that my visionary husband's lack of attention to detail is a major character flaw.

After retrieving the bag, our recalculated route from the hotel took us to the highway's end, lined up for a ferry. This wasn't in the plan.

"Yes'm, ma'am," said the gentleman when I asked, "Are we really getting on a boat, here, and is it really the fastest route?"

It happened to be Father's Day, and the father next to me in the driver's seat was a sailor at heart. Nate loves the water and comes alive on a boat. In one year he'd read twenty novels about sea adventures. This whole detour wasn't his fault. It was his gift.

Nate's mistake led us into a mini-adventure as we sat in our Suburban on a boat cruising the coastal inland waters of Virginia. This was for him.

We work to avoid the mistakes that God turns around and uses to show us His tender nearness. He leans in to reach us in the midst of what we are tempted to resent.

Sometimes God teaches me through my circumstances, things for which I develop an eye as I adore and sometimes through my adoration, so that I might look for Him this way, later, tucked away in my circumstances.

AND HERE, IN THE MIDDLE MINUTES, WE ADORE

USING MATTHEW 15:32

Father, You feel.

The people whom You made move Your heart.

I am one of them, even (especially) on that day. I am fixed on You and wondering, "Who is this man?" yet trapped in all my humanity. And You have compassion on me.

You don't see with Your eyes in a way that puts distance between You (perfect) and what You have created (weakened in flesh), but You see them with eyes that receive them.

I adore You, compassionate God, who is tender with me.

You receive me—all of me. My burps and hiccups and hunger—all signs of my flesh—were, once, worn by You. And You, who could master them all, look at me with gentle understanding.

You saw every face in that crowd that served to mask the layers of who they really were. You saw external scrapes, cuts, and bruises, and internal torrents. You carried it all. And You responded with compassion. You entered what they were experiencing. You leaned in.

You gave of Your tenderness to that crowd, just as You give of Your tenderness to me now.

My weakness stirs You. The parts of me that I despise, the reminders of this temporal body of death, move You on my behalf. You love me, even in my humanity. Especially in my humanity.

My humanity invokes Your compassion, God.

When I am me, weak, You reveal Yourself as both strong and tender.

You are not annoyed by me or my temporality. You are soft toward me.

My frailty—in You—isn't to be despised; it's to be carried to that place at Your feet where my life releases the bow I was made to give and You write Your name on all that I am not.

I adore You, God of compassion, who turns what is parched and hungry and strapped by my limitations into a glory in which I can participate.

You make me beautiful by Your tenderness.

TENDER GOD, GENTLE WITH ME

Psalm 18:35 | Psalm 23:1–2 | Psalm 34:18 | Psalm 36:7 | Psalm 42:8 | Psalm 45:2 | Psalm 57:10 | Psalm 63:3 | Psalm 103:4 | Psalm 103:8 | Psalm 103:10 | Psalm 119:77 | Psalm 143:8 | Song of Solomon 2:3 | Isaiah 40:11 | Hosea 11:4 | Matthew 8:2–4 | Matthew 15:32 | Matthew 20:34 | Luke 1:78–79

TINY (BIG) PRAYERS

"The Lord is merciful and gracious" (Ps. 103:8).
"Your lovingkindness is better than life" (Ps. 63:3).
"Your mercy reaches unto the heavens" (Ps. 57:10).

DIALOGUE WITH HIM

How do you envision God's response to you when you sin and return to Him or when you fail (perhaps even like in my story when Nate's mistake of leaving behind his bag was purely that—a mistake)?

Consider the times in your day when you've sinned and what your typical response is to that sin. Notice, in yourself, your stance toward God when you fail or miss a self-imposed standard. Do you see Him as He is revealed in His Word?

Identify a recent instance when you struggled to see Him as tender, and ask Him to reveal to you, through His Word in the verses listed in the "Tender God, Gentle with Me" section, what His true response was to you in that moment. Adore Him through those verses.

This week or this day, ask Him to show you how these failures are more about who He is as tender and gentle with you than who you are not in your failings. Write it down when it happens. Adore, then.

16 | MAJESTIC GOD

You are more glorious and excellent
than the mountains of prey.

—PSALM 76:4

IN THE GRIT

When I was growing up, we spent fifty-one weeks of the year
dreaming about our one week at the ocean. I have intermittent memories of elementary school projects, friendships
in my early years, and family reunions, but I can still feel
the grit of sand against the sunburned skin on my back and
smell the scents of suntan lotion and summer sweat com-
mingling in the air around me. The potent memories from
the beach stand out in front of the blurred in-between days
of childhood.

That year-long anticipatory wait set me up to see the
beach as a haven. Or perhaps seeing it as a haven built a
year of anticipation. I felt safe at the beach. Alive and received in my girlhood. Unbound. Free to marvel at the
ocean, which was much bigger than my travel radius back
home. More exciting than the movie theater, the ice cream
shop, and the mall was this wild, deep expanse still tethered
to the tidal rhythm.

In my twenties when I built my days around my youth ministry, impassioned to share the gospel with teenagers who didn't know Jesus, the beach became a different kind of safety to me. This time I needed to flee. I sighed with relief as I left behind the home where most of my ministry happened. The heaviness I revisited when I returned home confirmed the beach to be my escape.

Home bound me to responsibility and expectations. I lived carefully. Measured. Calculated, even. My passion for God had a ceiling, one I felt but didn't identify until much later. At home He seemed more watchful and cautionary, guiding and directing me. At the beach, He felt untamed and expansive, like the ocean. I endured the ministry-focused God I knew back home for fifty-one weeks and looked forward to engaging with Him in the wild for that one.

As I reflect on most of my earlier years with God, the moments I encountered a person—a calloused-handed man, an attuned Father—often happened in the outdoors. At age fifteen, under a star-spangled Michigan sky, I invited Him into my life. Later, at Saranac Lake in upstate New York, as water lapped against the rocks on which I sat and looked at the outline of the Adirondacks, I decided I didn't want to follow Him casually but wanted to give the entirety of my life over to Him. Later still, as I walked along the dunes of Hilton Head Island in South Carolina at sunset, I admitted defeat, admitted that the way I approached God and myself left me exhausted.

Away from the hum of air conditioning or the roar of cars racing the clock to their destinations, God's majesty seemed accessible. In the wild, He didn't have a clipboard in hand, assessing my productivity. He made the screech owl and the coyote and the blazing sunset that vanished into dusk. His attributes felt nearer to me outside my front door than at my desk.

On the last morning of an unusually extravagant Maui getaway with Nate, my measurement of the week centered around two surprise rainbows, quiet morning runs along the water, and the electric sunsets of Hawaii. I held deep gratitude for this unexpected week, and I couldn't talk to Him without noting the way He showed off to me. It was as if He was saying, *You came here to find Me, Sara. And you did.*

My body's inertia wanted to return to the habit I'd developed over the years—dreading the day I left the beach. And I wanted to sink into despondency over the fifty-one weeks ahead, where I exchanged shooting stars for text messages and the rolling ocean tides for simulated noisemakers in our children's bedrooms, where I extrapolated lessons on good Christian living from sermons and podcasts instead of falling asleep in wonder at how near He had been in one single day.

The sad sank in for just a minute before He caught my attention. Psalm 76:4 happened to be my place of adoration that day: "You are more glorious and excellent than the mountains of prey."

Oh, the irony, reading this and adoring Him as I watched the clouds hang, ominous, over the volcano in the distance. He was better than my view.

When my toes sink into the sand at the edge of the ocean, when I'm whale watching in Maui, when the sun sets the trees behind our home ablaze with light, what I'm seeing is a shadow. It is a shadow of Him.

These things don't replace Him; they draw my eyes away from me and into the glorious majesty of the one who made them.

My adoration that morning gave context for the passion stirring inside of me during our week in Hawaii and for the passion ignited in me when I was a seven-year-old girl sharing a raft with my dad at the ocean.

We humans need a proxy, and He lights the world with His majesty to draw our eyes up to see its source.

In adoration, "one's mind runs back up the sunbeam to the sun" (C. S. Lewis).

His beauty in creation serves a purpose: to give us a taste for the majestic. Just like when we drove through the night to reach the beach year after year, when we taste His majesty, we want more.

The ocean incited my hunger for the wild and unbound nature of God, but the sea would never be enough to quench that hunger.

As I adored overlooking the Maui shoreline that last morning, I realized that majesty was coming home with me and that this week was merely a taste, intended to make me hungrier.

AND HERE, IN THE MIDDLE MINUTES, WE ADORE

FROM PSALM 76:4

You are the majestic one, but I often stop at the sunbeam.

You alight Yourself in my world because Your majesty is limitless, but my eyesight and my perspective often keep me bound. I see You as clean

*and tidy and measured, but adoring You as majestic
expands my vision. It makes me look up. I see wide
and long and far and deep into what You created,
and into You, when I adore You as majestic.*

*I adore You for expanding my perspective on You
and on the world. I adore You for alluring me
through what I see in front of me. I adore You,
majestic God, for being unsearchable in Your
majesty.*

*You show Yourself off, to me, because I was made to
know the limitlessness of Your nature. I feel small,
and You lift my eyes away from me and onto Your
majesty. You are big; You take me away from myself
and lift my eyes onto You.*

I adore You, majestic God.

MAJESTIC GOD

Exodus 15:11 | 1 Chronicles 29:11–12 | Psalm 19:1–4
| Psalm 29:3–4 | Psalm 63:2 | Psalm 68:35 | Psalm 76:4 |
Psalm 77:14 | Psalm 104:1–2 | Psalm 110:3 | Psalm 145:5–7
| John 5:20 | Revelation 22:16

TINY (BIG) PRAYERS

"Who is like You?" (Ex. 15:11).
"The voice of the LORD is powerful" (Ps. 29:4).
"You are very great" (Ps. 104:1).
"I will meditate on the glorious splendor of Your majesty"
(Ps. 145:5).

Your starting point for discovering His majesty may not be like mine. Perhaps nature and the world outside have not been your window into His bigness. Take a few minutes to consider the last time He felt significant and larger than life and too big to comprehend.

How did you feel at that moment? How did you receive Him as He revealed Himself to you in that way? How did it change you?

If that last question is difficult to answer or the time when you brushed up against His majesty feels distant, adore Him from a particular area in your life that feels bound or small or confined. For example, at times the monotony of the rhythms of the toddler and baby life can leave me feeling bound to the small. Instead of reaching for something bigger in that place, I ask Him to show Himself as majestic in those moments. Choose three or four verses by which to adore Him in the following week in that place that feels small or as you consider that place that feels small.

If you notice that exploring His majesty is a strength of yours (some of us are more inclined to consider the magnitude of God's beauty and glory), then utilize the adoration verses to expand your explorations.

17 | MY FRIEND

Behold, I stand at the door and
knock. If anyone hears My voice and
opens the door, I will come in to him
and dine with him, and he with Me.

—REVELATION 3:20

IN THE GRIT

On vacation, all your dreams come true. I page through travel magazines in the waiting room of the dentist's office. In them I see still, clear water, friendly dolphins, exquisite cottages with verandas that open to sheaths of white sand and oceans at low tide for miles. The breeze whisks through sheer white curtains and windows with no screens. (There are no bugs on this vacation.) A single glass of chardonnay sits beside a novel.

I roll my eyes as if I don't buy this dreamy yet unrealistic outlook.

I still must carry some vestige of that dream, though, because we are three days into our annual family beach trip and the rainy day feels depressing. I ignore the extra hours with family and the free space to read and the pool outside our door to replay all that went into packing for a family of, now, eight. The clouds mirror my mood—or perhaps they inform it.

I escape for a few minutes when the rain lifts to take a walk on the beach, just me and my grumpy heart. Lost in my head, I stare mostly at my feet as they make depressions on the rain-drenched sand. For a second, I look up. At that moment, the clouds part and the sun peeks through. It's captivating, the blue of another world breaking through the dark gray of low-hanging clouds on a rainy day. In one small opening, I see the bright, radiant summer sky. I see the sun and possibility and beauty.

Then, in a flash, the clouds reconvene, forming again the universal gray.

Had I not looked up, I would have missed it.

He got my attention. I began to adore. I was learning that adoration could speak into the everyday minutes. I felt glum, but He winked at me through His creation. All that this vacation lacked weighed on me—no novels completed, no hours of quiet staring out at the serene ocean.

But He saw me. He saw this one seemingly insignificant, grumpy moment. And He showed Himself to me through the break in the clouds.

I adored back to Him: *Thank You, God, for declaring Yourself in the sky. I adore You for showing up in this isolated minute that felt like one to overlook and ignore. Thank You for making significant what felt insignificant.*

This is friendship—communicating over the minutes. He saw me. He responded. I saw Him. I responded. My insides got a lift because of His presence.

And later in the day, the clouds broke in more than just that one spot. They folded like a curtain to reveal the summer behind them. Two different landscapes tucked inside one day, one beach.

They spoke to me of this ongoing friendship. He, available. I, responsive. He, seeing. I, being seen and received and responding.

God is playful. Even on our grumpy days.

Especially on our grumpy days.

AND HERE, IN THE MIDDLE MINUTES, WE ADORE

FROM REVELATION 3:20

You wait for me as a friend. Voice ready, at the door, available. God, You are the available friend, ready to step into any single minute of mine.

I adore You for not seeing any minute as insignificant but being ever available to the slightest movements of my insides.

You stand at the door and You knock. You wait for my response. You patiently wait for my response. And in Your waiting You are available. I adore You for being my friend. Present, near, waiting.

Ready for my receiving.

I adore You for waiting for my receiving.

I adore You for Your gentle friendship, accessible to me where I am.

MY FRIEND

Exodus 33:11 | 2 Chronicles 20:7 | Proverbs 22:11 | Song of Solomon 5:16 | Isaiah 41:8 | Matthew 26:50 | John 3:29 | John 15:12–15 | John 17:23 | John 21:12 | James 2:23 | James 4:4 | James 4:8 | Revelation 1:1 | Revelation 3:20

TINY (BIG) PRAYERS

"Greater love has no one than this, than to lay down one's life for his friends" (John 15:13).

"And he was called the friend of God" (James 2:23).

"I stand at the door and knock" (Rev. 3:20).

DIALOGUE WITH HIM

To consider God as a friend requires most of us to think outside of our normal way of relating to Him. For this character trait of God, I encourage you to read through each of the verses and, as you do, ask God to surface the questions you have about Him as a friend. Allow yourself to wrestle, not to merely accept my words or suggestions but to seek out what His Word says about Him as a friend.

Then, select one verse that speaks to your spirit about Him as a friend and take that with you, throughout your week. Whether on a notecard or in a journal or with your Bible propped open on your kitchen counter, adore Him as friend during the times when you might converse with a friend. Freshly consider Him. Invite Him as a friend into places in your heart, life, and day where you have not invited Him before. Open your insides to receive Him as a friend and reach back to Him (who is also able to receive His people's friendship) in response.

18 | MY PROTECTOR

He is a shield to those who put their trust in Him.

—PROVERBS 30:5

IN THE GRIT

I like to be right. More infuriating than being wrong is when I know I am not wrong and yet I get accused of being wrong. This dogged eye for justice (if I were to frame it positively) weathered small hits in my younger years.

My senior year of high school, a large group of us played a harmless prank on our rival high school. At two in the morning, youthful zeal and trunks full of spray paint collided in poor decision making by a handful of those in our group. Three in the morning found all of us under the fluorescent lights of our high school's administration offices. Our principal gave us each a slip of paper and asked us to write down the names of those who moved this harmless prank toward permanent damage.

I speculated who did and heard the chatter on the way back to our school, but I had never set eyes on the vandals during their crime, so I left my paper blank. One of the wrongdoers—one of my friends—decided that I, the Christian in the group, was the informant. For the remainder of my senior year, he spent countless hours retaliating for what he thought I did.

I seethed on the inside, knowing who turned him in—not me—and receiving his false accusations while those who did turn him in chose not to reveal themselves. Why would they want to after seeing what I endured?

I didn't see this as the preparation it was. More practice came after those youthful years—stories too painful and too personal to share in these pages, of feeling unprotected and vulnerable to the false accusations of others who were determined to blame someone.

Though I don't often fear things that go bump in the night, I do fear an inaccurate perception of me that might lead to an accusation. And as happens so often with our fear, since that moonlit night on the front field of my rival high school, He has given me many opportunities to see that His perfect love overrules fear.

But first I have to feel the gap that even my best efforts toward shielding myself leaves. My strongest self-preservation tactics still leave me exposed.

One afternoon I felt the nakedness of standing, unshielded, with my accuser. For weeks I had crafted arguments in my head about why this person's harsh words about me were unfounded—wrong, ill-delivered, unsafe, and unfair. I repeated what I would say if given a chance. I defended myself in my head repeatedly. But it didn't work. I still felt weak and exposed. I again cried at the words spoken about me, even though I knew the voice delivering them was faltering and wounded, hampered. I still wanted to retaliate.

I had no shield, no chance against the accusations. And

in my emotional state, I constantly repeated the words slung at me and re-formed the argument I would never give in response.

I needed another way.

I spent too much time protecting myself from those words already spoken. I finally relented. I adored.

Through Proverbs 30:5—"He is a shield to those who put their trust in Him"—I adored what I wasn't believing or living out.

I didn't see a need for a shield until I saw the flaws in my shield. I didn't ask for a protector until I felt the nakedness of not reaching for His protection. I didn't know this side of Him until I adored.

I knew the damage of this independence at seventeen, and that well-trodden path allowed me in my thirties to exercise the same independence before I thought to ask Him to be my shield.

Until I no longer wanted to be independent.

Adoration initiated a new leaning.

AND HERE, IN THE MIDDLE MINUTES, WE ADORE
FROM PROVERBS 30:5

You shield me. You protect what I fiercely guard. You overrule my best strategies with the protection found in Your person.

You deliver. You build a shield around me. You preserve me. You are my defense, God.

In sight of Your face, I let down my defenses, and I receive the protection that makes me safe. I receive

*You, God, my protector. I adore You as the one who
disarms me. I need no arms in Your presence. You
shield me from every single hurt.*

*I adore You, my preserver. My maintainer. You do
the work, and I rest in You. I find myself in You as I
rest under Your protection.*

MY PROTECTOR

2 Samuel 22:2–4 | Psalm 5:12 | Psalm 9:9 | Psalm 16:8 |
Psalm 23:4 | Psalm 31:2 | Psalm 46:1 | Psalm 59:16–17 |
Psalm 60:11–12 | Psalm 62:6–8 | Psalm 91 | Psalm 121:5–8
| Psalm 125:2 | Psalm 144:2 | Psalm 145:20 | Proverbs 30:5
| John 17:15 | Romans 8:31 | 1 Thessalonians 5:23 | 2 Thes-
salonians 3:3

TINY (BIG) PRAYERS

"God is a refuge for us" (Ps. 62:8).
"The LORD is your keeper" (Ps. 121:5).
"My fortress, my high tower and my deliverer" (Ps.
144:2).
"He is a shield to those who put their trust in Him"
(Prov. 30:5).

DIALOGUE WITH HIM

Some of us face overt threats. I didn't seek God as my protector until I received a threat against my safety. It's human nature to self-protect. Our inclination toward self-preservation
creeps undetected into many areas of our lives. Even those
of us who haven't faced threats can relate to our urge to
preserve.

Consider these questions:

- When you felt misunderstood, how did you respond?
- When someone wrongly accused you or judged you, what did you think? What did you do?
- When your sense of value or worth—in your work or your motherhood or fatherhood or a role you carry—was challenged, what was your response?

We become experts at protecting ourselves and, as a result, miss the safety of His protection. As you consider Him as a protector, think of one area of your life where you are working hard to protect yourself. Commit that area to adoration. Choose one of the verses in the "My Protector" section and adore Him now as protector. Carry the verse with you and be watchful. When you notice yourself scurrying to defend or preserve or protect yourself, adore in that minute.

19 | CELEBRATORY GOD

> Because You have been my help,
> therefore in the shadow of Your
> wings I will rejoice.
>
> —PSALM 63:7

IN THE GRIT

At twenty and fiery for God, I did not reach for a life of ease. Nate and I didn't include ease in our early talks about our vision for our marriage and family. To the contrary, we wanted to challenge the cultural clamor for comfort. We liked being different. We made decisions against ease and conventionality.

But after I turned forty, I caught myself daydreaming a new version of ease, sizing up those who had smaller families, fewer hearts in the balance, less opportunity to make a mess of things. Of course smaller does not equate with a life of ease, but in my desperation, this was my perception.

I found myself treating every hangnail as if I'd lost a limb, the craving for ease simmering and gaining strength. The babe not napping made me despondent. Children squabbled and I snapped. In one week we had several appliances break, and I choked back tears talking to the repairman.

My vision for my life didn't include a reach for ease, but my daily minutes did.

It culminated in an evening walk with Nate along the Pacific Ocean. I wanted to talk strategy and planning regarding a certain area of our lives, and he was reluctant. "We aren't there yet," he said. My response lacked understanding of why he felt this way, and it lacked trust in his discernment. We argued as we did in our early married days, forgetful of one another, forgetful of how to graciously handle conflict, lost in the disagreement. All of this at our beachside getaway. I went to bed wondering when that magical day when everything happens as you expect it to might come.

Having a vision for a life of uncomfortable reach for God doesn't preclude you from clamoring for ease.

The next morning, I sat on the veranda overlooking the cerulean blue of the ocean as people stood on the shore watching for whales, and I adored Him through Psalm 63:7. With no intent to have adoration touch the part of me that felt disgruntled and distant from my husband and hurt by God, who seemed to continue to allow subtle misfortunes to impact my perfectly planned day, I randomly selected this verse. Like a pouting child in front of a sandcastle, I felt it my right to stew in the middle of this vacation.

But His Word, as Hebrews 4:12 tells us, doesn't dance around the periphery.

"For the word of God is living and powerful, and sharper than any two-edged sword, piercing even to the division of soul and spirit, and of joints and marrow, and is a discerner of the thoughts and intents of the heart."

Even in my passive engagement, God is active.

Adoration alerted me to Him.

In my subconscious, I believed ease brought joy. When the children complied in an ordered house and friends showed up for big events in my life and marriage had no conflict, I would throw my head back and laugh with joy at my life.

This vision of rejoicing paled in comparison to what Psalm 63:7 offered me in adoration.

"Because You have been my help, therefore in the shadow of Your wings I will rejoice" (Ps. 63:7).

Rejoicing comes in the shadow of His wings. Joy comes when He helps us. Thus, joy comes when we need help.

As I adored, using words I didn't believe and feeling frustrated, I arrived at this notion: rejoicing is the fruit of being helpless and having Him help. Thus, joy is possible when the air conditioning breaks. His impartation of joy is available to ones like me who need help, who are tired of daydreaming a life that isn't theirs, who want something different out of their current minute.

My morning turned as I considered Him.

Reading this, you may think that it all seems simple: a few minutes of adoration sprinkled on a tough day and everything looks brighter. Some rare days it is that simple, but these vignettes tell of the tipping point. Our oceanside getaway came after a year of adjusting to six children and the nine months before that, my feeling physically limited by pregnancy at an older age. Nearly two years of joy had evaded me. Asking God about this discontentment in my heart, I turned a corner that Psalm 63:7 morning.

Adoration and inviting God into my story, along with

the history that led me to this moment, frequent exploration of His Word, and stillness often make for a tipping point.

These stories tell of the shift, the infusion of faith: *He can alter our insides.*

I returned home with sand in my suitcase, gifts for the children, and expectancy. This God who imparts joy also celebrates Himself, in me. There is an exchange that moves beyond the flat tire or the child's sickness or the lost file at work and into the deeper parts of me that He intended for communion with Him in the shadow of His wings.

AND HERE, IN THE MIDDLE MINUTES, WE ADORE

FROM PSALM 63:7

You help. You give joy. You celebrate Yourself in me and the nearness we have when I come underneath Your wings.

I don't like to need help. Drawing near requires me to need a nearness, and I find comfort in self-sufficiency.

But You draw me through the hiccups in life. You meet me in what feels to be hurdles, ones You have allowed so that You can redirect me to You.

I adore You, God with wings under which I find joy. I adore You for giving joy in the unlikely places of my life. I adore You for offering generous help, the kind that changes me.

I adore You for being the designer and imparter of joy on my insides.

CELEBRATORY GOD

Psalm 5:11 | Psalm 16:11 | Psalm 21:1 | Psalm 21:6 | Psalm 30:5 | Psalm 30:11–12 | Psalm 45:7 | Psalm 51:8, 12 | Psalm 63:7–8 | Psalm 89:15–16 | Psalm 105:3 | Psalm 126:1–6 | Isaiah 61:3 | Jeremiah 31:13 | Matthew 25:21 | John 15:11 | Hebrews 1:9 | Hebrews 12:2 | 1 Peter 1:8–9 | Jude 24

TINY (BIG) PRAYERS

"In Your presence is fullness of joy" (Ps. 16:11).
"Joy comes in the morning" (Ps. 30:5).
"Restore to me the joy of Your salvation" (Ps. 51:12).
"That My joy may remain in you, and that your joy may be full" (John 15:11).

DIALOGUE WITH HIM

The verses listed in the "Celebratory God" section approach God as celebratory or speak to our need and desire for supernatural joy. Select which angle you need most right now— God as the one who celebrates what He made by putting Himself in you, or God who infuses joy in the unlikely minutes. Go through each verse and choose the ones that speak to that angle, and then adore. Give yourself days or a week to pay attention as you adore. What aspects of your life most resist His supernatural joy or Him as a God who is celebratory?

Think of one of those aspects and choose a few times while walking out that area of your life to adore Him in that moment. Let your adoration move from separate designated times of adoration and into the middle minutes.

Then at night before bed or in the morning after waking, reflect. How do you see your perspective on Him shifting?

20 | GOD WHO GIVES A SONG IN THE NIGHT

The LORD will command His lovingkindness in the daytime, and in the night His song shall be with me—a prayer to the God of my life.

—PSALM 42:8

IN THE GRIT

I live in Middle America. Every first Wednesday of the month at 10:00 a.m. we hear the sirens, a test of the tornado alert system. Once or twice a year we have a moment's notice to gather water and blankets and books before cramming ourselves into the basement bathroom to wait out the potential touchdown of a tornado. The decision making happens in seconds.

When we prepared to spend a month at the beach in my in-laws' home, I envisioned quiet evenings on the screened-in porch and long beach walks. I didn't think of hurricane season.

One week into our stay there, as Nate's parents traveled in China, the hurricane showed itself on the weather map. Neighbors talked on the sidewalks between houses about storm preparations. The lines at gas stations stretched into the streets. Grocery stores stocked their shelves with water and imperishables. This wasn't a split-second preparation; we watched the weather reports, hour by hour, between conversations for nearly a week about the advantages of staying or going.

We made reservations to evacuate out of state, then filled the bathtubs with water in case we stayed and lost access to our water source. Evacuating meant risking running out of gas on a crowded highway in 90-degree heat. Staying had its obvious risks. It all felt unfamiliar. Locals told stories of past storms and their decisions. Inexperienced, we prayed as men scaled the house to put up storm shutters.

One night, days before the storm hit, I sang to Virginia as I rocked her before bedtime, my ritual. Under heavy eyelids, her eyes shifted from staring at me to accepting the allure of sleep, cradled in safety. I sing the same old hymn to her every night still.

Though this was our every evening rhythm, my next morning's reflection made it feel fresh.

I adored through Psalm 42:8. It happened to be on my monthly list for that day—assigned unintentionally.

The LORD will command His lovingkindness in the daytime, and in the night His song shall be with me—a prayer to the God of my life.

The night felt real, ominous. The days before a hurricane turn dark as the storm approaches. We decided to stay, but with bags packed should the course of the storm make a last-minute shift.

I had experienced only one other hurricane. I was twenty-four, newly married, and three hours inland, staying with friends. Talking late into the night by candlelight after the power went out held a thrill.

Six children later, with the Sound at the edge of our neighborhood, I felt fearful in my honest moments and responsible.

Psalm 42:8 was the word for my honest heart.

I adored Him and fielded fear. The more I adored, the bigger my fear grew. I squelched it, silencing what I felt with lists of what to do to prep the house for the storm. In the quiet of adoration, I could feel my fear. But He didn't fear my fear, nor did it surprise Him.

The fear I was moderating grew to its actual size, thus my adoration had to grow with it.

God, Your Word says You command Your lovingkindness. I adore You for this lovingkindness. I need it in my desperation.

Your Word says Your song is with me. Thank You. I adore You for Your song. Can I hear it?

My mind went back to Virginia and the song I'd sung over her the previous night. I remembered how her chubby flesh began to sweat in my arms, her body drifting into the safety of sleep. My song and my presence were her security in the dark of night when lurking shadows can frighten the smallest ones.

His way with me is similar. His song pierces the dark of night. Over me. As I thought of Virginia and her security in light of Psalm 42:8, I knew it to be a hue of His song over me. If she can sleep under my song, I can sing under His.

That morning, adoration brought me to attention. I saw Him in my story. His Word secured me. He would sing over our storm, no matter where we were in it. And I could sleep or sing because of His song over me.

AND HERE, IN THE MIDDLE MINUTES, WE ADORE

FROM PSALM 42:8

You sing over me in my least expected hour.

I flinch at the night. I draw back because of the

shadows. I cower. And You sing. I fear, and You sing. I wander and You sing.

Your song is over me, surrounding me, with me in the darkest hour. I adore You for Your song, for Your presence, for You.

In the daytime, You secure lovingkindness, and in the night I can hear it through Your song. I am never alone. I adore You, God, for Your ever-always nearness. I praise You that I am never alone. Your song holds me. Your lovingkindness envelops me. I am Yours, safely kept in You.

I adore You for the song in the night.

GOD WHO GIVES A SONG IN THE NIGHT

Job 35:10 | Psalm 16:7 | Psalm 28:6–7 | Psalm 30:11–12 | Psalm 32:7 | Psalm 40:1–3 | Psalm 42:8 | Psalm 59:16 | Psalm 63:6 | Psalm 77:6 | Psalm 119:55 | Psalm 119:147 | Psalm 134 | Psalm 139:12 | Isaiah 24:14–16 | Isaiah 54:1 | Zephaniah 3:16–17 | Acts 16:25

TINY (BIG) PRAYERS

"You shall surround me with songs of deliverance" (Ps. 32:7).

"He has put a new song in my mouth" (Ps. 40:3).

"In the night His song shall be with me" (Ps. 42:8).

DIALOGUE WITH HIM

Identify an area or two that represent night to you—where you feel alone or afraid or tentative.

These are not always easy to access. If you cannot think of one, give yourself a day or two to observe your heart. When have you felt anxious? When do you find yourself tentative? When have you sought to fill space or time out of a fear of being alone? (Sometimes something as small as paying attention to when your heart races will give you a clue.)

Bring that area to Him—in the moment or the morning (or two) after—and identify what you feel when you are there. Write out those feelings in the form of a prayer, recognizing them before Him and inviting Him to help.

Then adore with this place in mind. Adore as it comes to mind, using the verses in the "God Who Gives a Song in the Night" section, and—if you are able—adore at that moment. If at night, consider keeping your Bible on your bedside table and adoring using one of the verses as you fall asleep. If you know of an impending dark moment, write out a few of these verses that resonate with that fearful place and prepare to step away and adore as you feel. (I have found solace in a side bedroom or restroom at a party or gathering, adoring God under my breath and enabling a greater ability to be present where I am after I do this.)

The place of safety I found in the story of the approaching hurricane was one I needed to return to several times each day before the storm. Adoration is a tether, bringing us back to Him as many times as we pull free. Let yourself be tethered as you feel.

Inviting God into our "big feelings," as we tell our children (and ourselves!), allows us to see Him as significant enough to field them.

21 | GOD WHO LIKES ME

The LORD takes pleasure in all he
has made!

—PSALM 104:31 NLT

IN THE GRIT

I don't like me today. I think I haven't liked me for a while.

The four children we adopted came to us with pre-conceived notions of what "Mom" meant. For all of them, "Mom" meant pain. Mom meant loss and ache and questions about themselves and God. Mom can still mean those things as they heal.

I glided into motherhood as an idealist. My bookshelves housed books on parenting and motherhood long before I flew across the ocean to become a mom. We took classes on parenting before we had a single child to carry our name. Vision drove me.

My mind, full of what Mom was supposed to mean, informed more than those early days of motherhood.

I teared up when Eden called me Mommy for the first time, her tiny brown hand cupped around the back of my arm, not letting go, just hours after I met her. Caleb could speak only a few words of English in his first few months with us. Mommy was one he used hourly.

My idealism, however, blinded me. I didn't anticipate the day when the painful understanding of Mom from their past might intersect with their relationship with me. My vision didn't fit around children who had trauma and pain in their history and a family melded as a result of that loss.

I kept trying to make my picture of Mom work with our reality and failed. I failed daily.

We moms are prone to dropping our jaws at the wounds others—past families or teachers or bullies or insecure friends—inflict on our children. But seeing how my idealism inflicted hurt, from my heart to our children, left me disdainful of myself.

And when we don't like ourselves, we do an excellent job of working ourselves into becoming more likable. That's what I did.

A mom who misses seeing her kids and attending to their hearts under her unrealistic and unbending vision, course corrects. I tended to their every need, seeking to catch every tear and validate each ache. *Don't miss a single moment,* was my mantra. *Make up for your failure.*

It is clear to me now—clear after my adoration—that when we feel unlikable, we compensate. We scurry to clean up our messes and do it better next time. We force our way into good behavior, into what people like, whether it be our spouses, our children, our bosses, or our parents.

I had been doing this for longer than I had been a mom, making myself a pro at being likable.

But when I adore Him as the one who takes pleasure in me, my gait softens. My shoulders unclench. I release relief in my breath. Failure sent me on a footrace toward better behavior when all He wanted was to receive me and all my failings.

I adore Him from Psalm 104:31, feeling unlikable, as if it's impossible for anyone to enjoy me. But His Word tells a different story of Him. He made me. He likes me. He sees Himself in me, this God who can wade through my murky insides to find something of Himself and something of beauty.

I adore Him from Zephaniah 3:17 as the God who likes me enough to rejoice over me with singing. He somehow finds something of worth in me that produces a song. And rejoicing. And gladness.

I come, feeling incapable, under the weight of my failure. He doesn't build me up, telling me the opposite of my assessment. His pleasure in me doesn't require me to give a peak performance or rest on false laurels from the self-medicated thinking that says, "Oh, you're not that bad." I come, having failed. And He still likes me. I come, aware of sin and mixed motives and fears, and He still likes me.

I can't believe this until I adore. Then I tell my heart that His Word holds a different story, a much better story, about His emotions toward me.

AND HERE, IN THE MIDDLE MINUTES, WE ADORE

FROM PSALM 104:31

You don't tolerate me; You take pleasure in me.

God, I know You love me. I've known this for a long time. But more than that, I am discovering how much You like me. You like what You have made.

I adore You for Your enjoyment of me. I adore You
that this is more than a partnership and more than a
handshake. You like what You see in me. You like what
You have made, enough so that You sing over me.

I don't like me, and You still like me. I reject me, and
You receive me, even in my failures. My flesh does not
threaten You. And You draw near. You like me.

I adore You for the safety You provide in Your kind
eyes and Your gentle receiving of me. I come to You,
again, as one who has failed because You make the
restoration of me safe.

GOD WHO LIKES ME

Psalm 16:3 | Psalm 17:8 | Psalm 104:31 NLT | Psalm 147:10–
11 | Psalm 149:4 | Proverbs 3:12 | Proverbs 11:20 | Song of
Solomon 2:4 | Isaiah 62:4 | Zephaniah 3:17 | Matthew 3:17 |
John 15:9 | Romans 5:8 | Romans 8:37–39 | Ephesians 3:14–
19 | Philippians 1:8 | 1 John 3:1 | 1 John 4:9–10

TINY (BIG) PRAYERS

"Keep me as the apple of Your eye" (Ps. 17:8).
"His banner over me was love" (Song 2:4).
"He will rejoice over you with gladness" (Zeph. 3:17).
"'As the Father loved Me, I also have loved you'" (John
15:9).

DIALOGUE WITH HIM

Consider a part of yourself that you don't like, a part that
feels detestable. Note how you respond to that part throughout the day. What do you do with what you don't like about

yourself? How have you resolved this dislike in your heart and life?

Now ask God to help you to bring this part of yourself to Him—not for evaluation or betterment but to be received by Him. In prayer, and as you adore using the verses in the "God Who Likes Me" section, bring all of this part of yourself to Him and ask Him to enable you to experience His receiving you. If the part of you that you don't like isn't a quirk but rather a sin, take time now to repent and ask Him to reveal to you His forgiving and receiving heart—to highlight the parts of you that He enjoys and in which He delights.

We often picture God as a stern parent or a hard coach. As you come to Him, let the Scripture—through your adoration—guide your image of Him, recognizing that your perspective may need some reworking.

Remember: adoration repairs the breach of our understanding of God. We struggle to believe that the God who loves us also likes us. Adoring through these verses is one of many steps toward mending that understanding.

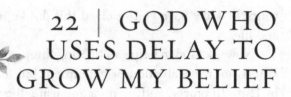

22 | GOD WHO USES DELAY TO GROW MY BELIEF

My soul, wait silently for God alone,
for my expectation is from Him.

—PSALM 62:5

IN THE GRIT

We've visited the same stretch of beach nearly every year for twenty-five years. There is not enough distance between visits for my memory to lapse. When I'm back at the beach, I can access being seventeen and adventuresome.

And every year there is one event that I scrapbook in my mind. Unfailingly, the happenings at the beach seem to mark the movement of God within my heart.

This year's mark went like this: The place we vacation is a tangle of beach homes and bike trails at the edge of an island. Some years we spend just as much time on our bikes as we do in the sand, zipping in and out of neighborhoods, scouting for alligators and egrets and blue herons, the exotic creatures we midwesterners don't see.

Two days into our trip and halfway through our evening family bike ride, one of the children slid farther and farther back from our group. We lightheartedly cheered her on, "inviting" her to keep up the pace, with no success.

She didn't budge.

This irritated me.

In the time that it took for me to slow down to where she was and let the others pass, I eked out a prayer: *Give me patience with her, Lord.*

So rather than chide her into keeping up with the others (something I've regretfully done in other areas of her life), I went her pace. We biked and talked. A little tenderness from me and her countenance lifted. (Having six people tell you to hurry doesn't do a soul well.) And then I realized that I wasn't only slow enough to see her—to look her in the eye and know that she just needed someone to be with her—but I was slow enough to hear Him. The setting sun lit the pond we passed. The bullfrogs sang in chorus. My little girl began to recover and even glow. Whether it was His creation speaking or Him, I don't know, but it called me to attention.

This moment was my annual beach whisper from God.

Weeks earlier, I had asked Him about an upcoming writing project, and the phrase that came to me as I prayed over days was this: "Grow slow."

Very little about life in the twenty-first century encourages the value of slow growth. The news and our Twitter feeds become dated after twenty-four hours. Babies learn to read and get potty-trained. Eight-year-olds can travel the country for select-team athletics. And Miracle Gro promises to produce buds on my roses within days.

None of these things, by themselves, is wrong. None. God can feed five thousand from one kid's lunch. He can speed growth.

But when we make the exception—fast and out-of-time growth—to be our standard for living, our souls can cave under the weight.

My puttering bike trip with the girl whose heart was reviving at the thought that she could "be" instead of having to keep in time and in step with her siblings was the picture of that phrase He'd given me—grow slow.

Slide the watch off your wrist. Open your eyes to the view along the way.

Grow slow feels hard to me when I peer at what others are doing. But it feels invigorating when I consider that the God of all time ordains my times and seasons—so when He says, *Grow slow*, the phrase promises growth. Grow slow isn't stagnancy; it's the true metric for endurance that our digital world doesn't heed. What I get when I wrestle with this invitation not to grow as the world grows but to grow slow is the revelation that my heart is much more patterned toward the timing and thinking of the world than I've ever acknowledged.

I have a subtle drive to grow big and fast. Here's how I can tell: I want our children to have the emotional dignity of thirty-five-year-olds when they're twelve and in (normal) conflict with each other. In my more frantic moments, I want my four-year-old to learn his letters (and now), and I want someone, anyone, to see (with maturity) the connection between the number of condiments they use on their eggs and our ever-increasing grocery bill.

When I look closely, no one under my roof seems to be growing fast and big. Could the daily frustrations I feel trace back to my expectation that the best things in life explode overnight, rather than sit in the beauty of the slow and steady (and profound and lasting) growth that God often desires?

God gives us the waiting room, yet I see that the waiting room is merely that for many: a place to sit and wait, restless.

He gave me the waiting room in my infertility, in my marriage, and dozens of times since—in events both big and small. Gritting my teeth and enduring or checking my watch felt natural. It's what you do in the waiting room. Yet this daughter, in this moment, opened me to hear His whisper, and I adored.

Psalm 62:5 tells me that my expectancy can grow in the waiting room. Against a world that speeds and a culture that tells me to hurry and an internal drive that measures my productivity, I adore through Psalm 62:5 and I stay on one phrase: *My expectancy is from Him.*

I unclench my fist as I adore. The memory of that bike ride brings back the smell of salty air. I replace the expectations I have for my task list and accomplishments with Him. My expectancy is from Him, I tell Him and my soul as I adore. The waiting room looks different. Purposed. He meets me in the waiting room as I adore. It doesn't feel so claustrophobic, so limiting. It feels expansive as I adore and imbibe His perspective on the waiting room. There is intention in that room.

In adoration, I revisit the truth that expands my insides, over and over again without shame.

AND HERE, IN THE MIDDLE MINUTES, WE ADORE

FROM PSALM 62:5

You use every minute of my delay to grow me. The waiting room is Yours to hold, to use, to fashion. Every halted circumstance, every thwarted minute,

every time my watch stops: You use it to grow my
insides, to grow my expectancy in You.

As my externals stall, You create an expectancy in
You within me.

I adore You, God of the waiting room. I praise You
for turning what is otherwise discarded into a place
where You grow me. I adore You for meeting me in
the waiting and changing me in the waiting.

I adore You for growing me slowly, God. Your way. I
adore You for Your way, God. The best way.

GOD WHO USES DELAY TO GROW MY BELIEF

Psalm 27:14 | Psalm 33:20–22 | Psalm 37:34 | Psalm 40:1–3
| Psalm 62:1 | Psalm 62:5 | Psalm 123:2 | Psalm 130:5–7 |
Isaiah 30:18 | Isaiah 40:31 | Lamentations 3:25–27 | Micah
7:7 | Romans 5:3–5 | Romans 8:23–25 | James 1:2–4 | James
5:7–8 | 1 Peter 1:6–8

TINY (BIG) PRAYERS

"Those who wait on the LORD shall renew their
strength" (Isa. 40:31).
"The LORD is good to those who wait for Him" (Lam.
3:25).
"I will wait for the God of my salvation; my God will
hear me" (Mic. 7:7).
"Let patience have its perfect work, that you may be
perfect and complete" (James 1:4).

DIALOGUE WITH HIM

My desire to heed His whisper, *Grow slow,* is not because I angle toward the small. It's the opposite. I want to see small fires of His heart spread everywhere across the earth into a raging blaze. (How's that for dramatic? It has been my prayer for years.) And I'm growing to trust Him enough to know that He put this desire within me, and so when He helps me to move in better step with His timing, I best listen. His way makes a harvest.

How about you? Where might He be "shackling" you with a slow biker to show you, in a picture or in a whisper, the timing He has for your current moment? Where is your waiting room? (Often it helps to identify it, rather than responding to it without naming it. Once we name it, we can ask for His presence there.)

Ask Him to prepare your heart to reclaim that room for Him. This is not a flippant decision nor is it a one-time decision; it is a progressive movement toward seeing what the world sees—and what you see—as waste through His eyes.

When you are ready (that doesn't mean when you are convinced; it means when you are prepared to unclench your fists and surrender this waiting room to Him), adore Him from that place. Ask Him to expand your insides to see what He sees there as you adore. Prepare to receive the waiting room in a new way.

23 | GOD WHO CHAMPIONS ME

> Likewise the Spirit also helps in our weaknesses. For we do not know what we should pray for as we ought, but the Spirit Himself makes intercession for us with groanings which cannot be uttered. Now He who searches the hearts knows what the mind of the Spirit is, because He makes intercession for the saints according to the will of God. And we know that all things work together for good to those who love God, to those who are called according to His purpose.
>
> —ROMANS 8:26–28

IN THE GRIT

Nate and I call it "the crazy place." The one or two or six scenarios that make our throats close and our minds narrow. We sweat, maybe pace, and either replay them or run from them, whichever is the best escape route from the crazy at the moment. They sabotage our thinking and our seeing.

Married to me for eighteen years, many of them spent laboring through rough patches of the heart, Nate will now put his hand on my elbow and say, "Babe, I think this is a crazy place for you." He calls me to attention when I can't do it myself. I do the same for him.

If I describe mine to you, you might encourage me to see things from another angle. You might apply Scripture or a personal story or gentle coaching to help me out of this spiraled thinking. None of these strategies are wrong—we need them at times. But acknowledging that each person has their unique crazy places, which seem normal and easy to navigate for others, may enable us to take a more exacting approach.

Unexpectedly, because of the need for an emergency trip, Nate and I scheduled two weekends away from our children in one month. This is neither our norm nor a goal; we both felt uncomfortable about the timing.

Days in advance of the first trip, I slid into my crazy place. All the walls against fear crumbled, as they often do in that rare place of my irrationality. I rehearsed scenarios in my mind. I practiced potentials and my responses. I lost days of face-to-face interactions with our children, entangled in my mind with the fear of all that might happen in my absence. Most crazy-place responses look irrational retrospectively, but have unstoppable energy behind them in the moment. Mine did.

I felt ill-equipped with little time to rest and two long packing lists to address. I did the only thing I knew might interrupt the force of negative energy. I adored.

Studying Romans at the time, I happened to be in Romans 8. In a way that only God could orchestrate (yet in a way He often does), at the height of my consuming fear, I landed on Romans 8:26–28 and considered Him as an intercessor—though most consideration in the crazy place, especially thoughts about God, is void. I can't even think about dinner.

209

Even with limited thinking and skepticism, I hovered there, demonstrating the power of habit.

I clung to one phrase and adored Him with it. I made it simple for my restless mind. *You help me in my weakness. You make intercession for me,* I adore-prayed from Romans 8:26. I didn't feel helped as I adored. I felt the spiraling. But adoration helps me to identify the spiral, and recognizing the spiral leads me to want help.

What Nate and I named the crazy place is not thinking before reacting and responding, contributing to a swirl that rarely enters conversation with God.

However, adoring from the crazy place can change the crazy place.

A new thought entered my mind as I adored: *I am not alone. Not only is God in it, but He is interceding for me in this place.* God prays for me when I cannot pray. Rarely do I think of my lack of prayer or my uninformed prayer as an opportunity to incite His praying for me.

This adoration opened me to consider this possibility. God prays for me! The truest champion intercedes in private.

I called on His attentiveness when I adored from that spiral. Adoration became the needed pause. I told my soul, *There's another way. It's His.* And His Word reached through what felt impenetrable.

Better than the best advice and even posting Scripture on your mirror is His Word cutting through the layers of fear, anxiety, and unthinking activity to reach your heart. Adoration is the inroad.

We went on both last-minute trips with all children unscathed. He met us on both.

Even better: He met me before I left.

AND HERE, IN THE MIDDLE MINUTES, WE ADORE

FROM ROMANS 8:26–28

*You champion me when I have no strength to
champion myself. I give up the fight, and You
continue what You started—all in the unseen realm.*

*You fight in the highest place, the place of power.
You intercede. You pray for me with knowing
prayers, and You champion me when I have nothing
left to parade. I crumble and You rise.*

*You fight for me when I'm frozen and when I have
lost. You win, on my behalf, every time.*

*You champion what You have made—me—so that
I need not defend myself. I rest in You, and You
champion me. I adore You, my greatest champion,
the one with power.*

GOD WHO CHAMPIONS ME

Exodus 14:13–14 | Psalm 3:3 | Psalm 34:5 | Psalm 37:6 | Psalm
60:12 | Psalm 63:7 | Psalm 118:6 | Psalm 144:1–2 | Proverbs
3:26 | Romans 8:26–28 | 2 Corinthians 2:14 | Hebrews 4:14–
16 | Hebrews 7:24–25 | 1 John 2:1 | 1 John 3:20

TINY (BIG) PRAYERS

"The One who lifts up my head" (Ps. 3:3).
"They looked to Him and were radiant" (Ps. 34:5).
"For the Lᴏʀᴅ will be your confidence" (Prov. 3:26).
"We have an Advocate with the Father" (1 John 2:1).
"The Spirit Himself makes intercession for us" (Rom. 8:26).

The term *crazy place* aside—some call it triggers, others say it's their place of fear or uncertainty—consider yours. Call it the name you feel most comfortable using. What, recently, has sent you into a spiral? When have you entered a place of fear or anxiety or shame that even the best encourager around you couldn't draw you out?

Let yourself feel what you felt at that time. Note those feelings, even your pulse as you consider it again. Pay attention to the inner workings of your heart.

Now bring those to God in adoration. Read through the verses in the "God Who Champions Me" section and select one or two that most resonate with your need for championing from that place, even if championing means fighting your fear for you. Adore Him as your greatest champion as you consider the situation that left your mind and heart sidelined.

Then ask Him to awaken Your senses to Him the next time you enter that place, whether through this same scenario or a different one.

Remember: the victory isn't in moving toward an unfeeling place or having full healing. The victory is communing with God in the place where we otherwise shut Him out.

24 | BEAUTIFUL GOD

The heavens declare the glory of God; and the firmament shows His handiwork.

—PSALM 19:1

IN THE GRIT

At ten on many spring, summer, and fall mornings, I tromp through the woods with Bo and Virginia. Homeschooling affords the unconventional hour outdoors for little ones. We walk a half-mile loop alongside our house, dodging grasshoppers, collecting acorns, scoping for a praying mantis, and measuring the progress of what feels to be miles of blackberry bushes.

I started doing this when I noticed how small hearts enlarge in nature. I kept doing it because I saw how big hearts come alive in nature.

Halfway through one of our fall walks, we took a side path down to the creek. We climbed over limbs and roots and steadied ourselves against trees as we walked down the steep slope. At the bottom, streaks of sun poked through the canopy of leaves, illuminating the cliff overlooking the creek.

Habit had Bo filling his hands and pockets with acorns

and rocks before we reached the bottom, ready to make a mark on the unpunctured water. Virginia stood between my legs, too cautious to explore, but curious and vigilant. Their preoccupation created a few minutes of silence for me.

I heard the wind—a gentle rustle. Branches moved inches. Millimeters, maybe. And one streak of sunshine reached across the side of Bo's face and his blond hair, enfolding him into nature's display.

In the ten minutes it had taken for us to walk to the creek, my mind was not present. I'd replayed a conversation with a friend, prioritized my tasks for the afternoon and evaluated whether I'd get them done, and chided myself for absently nodding my head at our children's discoveries along the way. *You know better,* said my internal critic.

The creek awakened my senses. Rather, He awakened my senses at the creek, slowing me to the cadence of the water trickling over the new rocks brought in by last week's storm, drawing my attention to the wind moving the branches, the sun dancing on the water and on Bo.

Then Scripture reminded me that He tells me His story out here. A phrase from Psalm 19 flashed through my mind: "The heavens declare the glory of God." The rest of the passage reads, "And the firmament shows His handiwork. Day unto day utters speech, and night unto night reveals knowledge. There is no speech nor language where their voice is not heard" (Ps. 19:1–3).

God can reach me in the woods in the middle of the morning if I let Him.

And if I can attend to the stillness and wonder I feel at a sun-streaked creek and trace that to the God-man behind it, I might consider that Jesus is beautiful too.

If He reaches into my world through drifting leaves and a sunbeam across blond locks, how must His face look?

I adore the God who is behind every stunning piece of nature, using it to allure me back to His eyes. As I do, with that one phrase that broke into my thinking—*The heavens declare the glory of God*—my task list and the conversation and my lack of productivity don't disappear, but they fade. They take their proper place.

AND HERE, IN THE MIDDLE MINUTES, WE ADORE

USING PSALM 19:1

God, You are beautiful.

You tell me about You, outside my door. You wait, beckoning me with the early sunrise and the sound of a mourning dove and the shout from a toddler, "Deer! Deer!"

You love revealing Yourself to me. If I can be wooed by a red moon or a woodpecker against the snow-lined branches, the lines on Your face, as I picture them, awaken me.

You looked up the tree to see Zacchaeus, and You stared into Your mother's eyes while you were on the cross. You reinstated Peter with Your knowing, tender expression as well as Your words.

Your face wears lines and definition. (God, You had a face!) You have laugh lines and piercing eyes. You roared with laughter and You wept.

I adore You, beautiful God—defining beauty for me

who craves but does not understand what she wants.
I adore You for clothing Yourself in humanity that I
might one day see Your face.

I adore You for declaring Yourself in the clouds and
the creek that I might explore Your beauty.

BEAUTIFUL GOD

Job 37:2–5 | Psalm 19:1 | Psalm 27:4 | Psalm 29:2 | Psalm 45:2 | Psalm 50:1–2 | Psalm 76:4 | Psalm 90:17 | Psalm 113:4–6 | Isaiah 6:3 | Isaiah 28:5 | Isaiah 33:17 | Hebrews 1:3 | Revelation 4:3 | Revelation 21:23

TINY (BIG) PRAYERS

"To behold the beauty of the LORD" (Ps. 27:4).
"You are fairer than the sons of men" (Ps. 45:2).
"The whole earth is full of His glory!" (Isa. 6:3).
"Your eyes will see the King in His beauty" (Isa. 33:17).

DIALOGUE WITH HIM

This one is simple. Take ten minutes this week to step outside and ask Him to show Himself to you. Write what you see, take it into your adoration, and use one of the verses in the "Beautiful God" section to adore back to Him.

If you're willing, consider two or three more ten-minute stints outside. All of our lives are habit forming, and our bodies crave the beauty that He created. I suspect you will find life outside your door. And I suspect as you receive His meeting you there, you will want to go again.

25 | GOD WHO RESPONDS TO MY CRIES

In the day when I cried out, You
answered me, and made me bold
with strength in my soul.

—PSALM 138:3

IN THE GRIT

This one day held incidental moments of aching strung together until dusk like clanging bells on my insides.

I snapped at the toddler, not so much because of his behavior as because of the text I received an hour earlier about the friend whose latest cancer scan showed signs of recurrence. That text hung in the backdrop of my day—*buzz*—as did the regret I had for my sharp tone and hurting child—*buzz*. I spent the late afternoon vacantly present, sautéing onions for dinner and sifting through the mail and ordering my mom a birthday gift, all while my mind spun. Three hours absent, yet a meal for (then) seven on the table, an extravagant birthday surprise in the mail, playdough distributed and manipulated and then swept off the floor.

My big kids felt the vacancy, and my littles communicated their needs through fusses. Everyone wondering, *Where is Mom today?*

By nine that night I was distant and hardened to myself. I was annoyed that even though I'm not a new mom, I'm still acting like one. I feared for my friend facing another cancer scare.

The fear for my friend triggered it all, but I didn't pay attention. Instead, I sank into a world of my own.

The crisp fall morning after called me to attention, something outside of me reviving me, as if awakened by ammonia. A flash of consciousness of my internal fears and anxieties and shame then gave pause for a moment to consider Him.

I looked back on the day before with different eyes—the sin, symptomatic, instead of its own beast. In my buried fear, I had snapped. In my concealed shame, I had recoiled. And after it all, I had condemned myself.

I'd related to Him as a distant and absent God. I hadn't seen the relationship between my suppositions of Him and my distance toward me, my hardness toward myself.

I knew enough to bring His Word into my flash of self-awareness. Adoration turns a self-aware moment into a holy encounter with God, no matter how messy.

Simple enough to dismiss, His tending is what my day needed. My day needed my cry to Him. My day required a reorientation around who He is when I cry out.

The internal ringing quieted, becoming less of a clang and more of a prayer, a series of prayers that went like this: *God, I'm afraid for my friend. I feel inadequate to mother our children. I feel shame over my lack and the responses I make when I'm weak. Please come.*

That last ask, coupled with His Word that tells me, "You answered me," and You "made me bold with strength in my soul" from Psalm 138:3, can change a minute. Adoration can change a minute.

I saw through the fog. With His Word, applied to my self-awareness, I saw Him. And I saw myself with more clarity. *I am weak, and He moves near me in my weakness. Underneath my impatience and shallow responses, there is a cry for help. When I do, and when I adore as I do, His Word fills the vacancy with a truth that felt elusive yesterday.*

I come crying (sometimes literally and sometimes with that gut-cry that says one word: "Help!"), and my God responds with Himself, strong enough to fill in all that I cannot.

In this adoration-prayer, I unclenched my mind from beholding lies about Him, and I allowed space to receive the truth of His Word. His Holy Spirit filled what had felt vacant just the day before. All as I adored.

I faced my friend's test results and my toddler's needs and my big kids' disappointment in yesterday's responses. Nothing had changed except for my mind and my heart.

And everything changed.

He heard me. I felt understood. He received me, and something inside of me shifted.

AND HERE, IN THE MIDDLE MINUTES, WE ADORE

USING PSALM 138:3

You hear me.

I squelch tears and push through my life. I fill my schedule and bide my time, riding over waves as if they're ripples, ignoring the torrent underneath me.

But ever so softly, You whisper, I'll hear You.

Your Word whispers to me in the night hours: He hears you, Sara. He hears.

You turn Your ear toward me. You are a ready listener. Not merely to listen but to hear, to see, and to respond. I adore You, God who listens. Who pauses at my life. Who has space in Your heart and Your magnanimous world to hear me.

I adore You that You respond to my weak cries with Your answers. Emboldening me, strengthening my weak places.

I come with hesitancy, and Your response is resounding. You tell me You are near and offer me Your ear—morning, noon, and night.

I adore You for listening. I adore You for Your attentiveness to the wanderings of my heart. I adore You for attending. Creator of the ocean tide and the humpback whale and the solar system, You attend to my weak cries. And in response, I adore.

GOD WHO RESPONDS TO MY CRIES

Exodus 3:7–8 | 2 Samuel 22:7–20 | Psalm 18:6–19 | Psalm 5:1–3 | Psalm 6:8–9 | Psalm 34:4, 17 | Psalm 40:1–2 | Psalm 55:16–18 | Psalm 61:1–2 | Psalm 65:5 | Psalm 104:34 | Psalm 116:1–2 | Psalm 138:3 | Psalm 145:18–19 | Isaiah 30:19 | Jeremiah 33:2–3 | Daniel 10:12 | Jonah 2:1 | Luke 18:1–8 | John 14:13–14 | John 15:7 | 1 Peter 3:12

"'Call to Me, and I will answer you'" (Jer. 33:3).
"My voice You shall hear in the morning, O LORD"
(Ps. 5:3).
"Hear my cry, O God; attend to my prayer" (Ps. 61:1).

DIALOGUE WITH HIM

Pick a middle minute from last week—an incidental or a
series of incidentals. An overlooked time that did not show
up on the report you gave to a friend or your mom or spouse,
but one that carried a tinge of anxiety. A flash of anger. You
took the chance to escape—a checked-out online scrolling
session, a binge, a hidden splurge.

And peer into that minute.

Before you ask Him for His thoughts, ask yourself. Map it
out if it helps. Start with that point on the map as your anxiety,
your anger, your escape, and then look around it. What went
undetected that led to that response (in some cases, that sin)?
Was it a text from a friend, a disappointment, some misunder-
standing, a sign of your failure showing up for others to see?

Now as you revisit, turn from the escape and turn it into
a cry out to Him. Take the pain that led to the sin or the response and hold it in your hand. Hold it out to Him. Be honest about what hurts and ask Him for a response. Don't wait
for a natural answer—the friend to understand you, the test
results to turn promising, the circumstantial ache to lift—ask
Him to meet you with Himself as you adore. Let adoration
crack you open. Don't hold back with your tears or your hurt
or your ache, and watch what His Word says about it as His
Holy Spirit moves through that Word to reach inside of you.

26 | MY PURSUER

The LORD is my shepherd; I shall not want.
He makes me to lie down in green pas-
tures; He leads me beside the still waters.
He restores my soul; He leads me in the
paths of righteousness for His name's sake.

—PSALM 23:1–3

IN THE GRIT

I schedule dentist appointments, do the grocery shopping and meal planning, cleanse gravel-embedded wounds, and research learning assessment tests. I spend so much time initiating as an adult that sometimes I forget: God made me to be a forever-child.

One day into the new year, fresh with expectancy, I became the family nurse. Influenza left us quarantined—each kid to their room for days while I traveled with supplies and food from one bedroom to the next, until I took sick. It lasted six weeks before we rid our house and our bodies of the flu. It was February before I remembered the fleeting expectation and fervor of January 1 with that vague sense of something lost, irretrievable.

My crew depended on me for nearly everything. New supplements, digestible food, cold compresses, sometimes help on their way to the bathroom. Around the clock I initiated. "It's time for more elderberry syrup, sweetheart." "Have you eaten anything yet?" "Let's check your temperature." Multiplied by six.

I didn't fear their deaths or their taking a turn for the worse, but I felt the weight of unceasing responsibility. Even when I got sick, during the daytime hours when Nate was at work, someone needed to be in charge.

Being in charge to that degree shriveled my insides temporarily. It revealed and exacerbated what I felt the other non-influenza-struck days of the year: it all depends on me.

The flu gave me more than six weeks of a household infirmary; it gave me a mirror into my heart. Lying in bed as kids moaned upstairs in pain, I thought, *Somewhere inside I don't trust anyone but me.*

The spirited conversations with God when we feel strong and capable take on a different flavor when He reveals Himself as He always is—our only option.

God pursued me in the bleak midwinter by allowing me to realize the unfamiliarity of shepherding, the awkwardness I felt by His pursuing me.

We say the words of psalms like Psalm 23 as if they're poetic and not painful. But I work hard not to be a sheep in need. I work hard not to be in want. I plan meals and make provision in my mind for any difficult eventuality. I resist what would make me need shepherding, unaware that what my heart longs for most is to be pursued.

He intends to lead me. But it's not until I can no longer initiate on my own or my responsibilities exceed my capabilities that I ask what pursuit looks like, what it means to be His sheep. To lean into that little girlhood again.

AND HERE, IN THE MIDDLE MINUTES, WE ADORE
FROM PSALM 23:1–3

You pursue me. When I'm tired or reach my limit, You pursue me. Before I even start, You pursue me. At the front and back ends of my life, You pursue me.

You shepherd my resistant soul.

I adore You, God, my pursuer. I adore You for shepherding a sheep as resistant as I am. I adore You for knowing when I need rest or a cold drink or the refreshing that only You can bring. I adore You for leading me.

You pursue and You reach me. You find me in my strength and You shepherd me toward Yours. My obstinacy does not threaten You. You tame the parts of me that need leadership and draw me, gently, under Your pursuit. I run, and You follow.

You chase me, God. With my circumstances and my life, You track me.

And You find me. The end of Your pursuit is me, and once You find me, You bring me into the safety of being Yours.

I adore You, my pursuer.

MY PURSUER

Deuteronomy 31:6 | 2 Chronicles 16:9a | Psalm 23:1–3, 6 | Psalm 95:6–7 | Psalm 119:133 | Psalm 139:5–6 | Ezekiel 34:11–12 | Luke 15:4 | Luke 19:10 | John 4:23 | John 15:1–2 | John 15:16 | John 15:26 | Acts 17:26–27 | Romans 8:27 | Philippians 1:6 | 1 Thessalonians 5:23–24 | Hebrews 12:26b–29 | 1 John 4:19 | Revelation 3:20

TINY (BIG) PRAYERS

"Surely goodness and mercy shall follow me" (Ps. 23:6).
"You have hedged me behind and before" (Ps. 139:5).
"I chose you" (John 15:16).
"He who has begun a good work in you will complete it" (Phil. 1:6).

DIALOGUE WITH HIM

Identify two or three areas of your life where you are the initiator. What does it feel like for you to be the initiator? What is your heart's response to your frequent initiation? How have you seen Him allowing you to struggle as you initiate—to potentially bring you into an awareness of being pursued?

Consider whether you can relinquish one of those areas where you initiate—perhaps an inconsequential one, as practice. For example, I recently chose to let go of speaking to one of the children related to a heart issue I wanted them to address. Instead, I asked Him to move in them as I remained silent and prayerful.

Ask Him to show you His pursuit of you as you divert your attention away from initiating. Select one verse from the "My Pursuer" section to linger on as you relinquish initiating, as you wait on His pursuit and His leadership. When you feel anxious about letting go, thank Him for His pursuit. Ask Him to expand your heart in such a way that you can be led, even more, by Him as the pursuer.

A thought to consider: What do you lose by allowing yourself to feel the weakness of being pursued? What might you gain?

27 | GOD WHO REACHES DEEP

But whoever drinks of the water that
I shall give him will never thirst. But
the water that I shall give him will
become in him a fountain of water
springing up into everlasting life.

—JOHN 4:14

IN THE GRIT

"We assumed you couldn't make it, but wanted to make sure you knew you were invited," she said.

Her intentionality softened the sting. She was right; I couldn't make it.

At the moment I received this last-minute invitation to circle up with the dearest of friends and find reprieve from my daily life, my house looked like this:

Bo and Virginia had sprawled themselves across my office floor, constructing a home out of an oversized box. Intermittent squabbles and squeals left me unsure of whether it was time to switch to a new game.

Lily practiced her violin in the same room as Hope—not far from the littles' squeals—as Hope finished her math assignment. I noticed them for a second before hearing

Caleb's call for help. He couldn't find his lacrosse jersey, and Coach Nate would be home in minutes to drive him to practice. Eden intercepted my looking with a question about her literature assignment.

Ten minutes passed before I heard the plumber at the door, which somehow alerted me to the smell of spaghetti sauce burning, not simmering, on the stove.

I greeted Meryl at the door and showed him to the clogged sink, then ran to save dinner.

Stirring the pot reminded me of the dinner invitation I couldn't accept. Life with this many kids meant a lot of last-minute shifts, but not often a change that wasn't a fire drill.

In a house full of people, I felt lonely this night.

What I now know to be true of every mother, and of every person, that no two stories and experiences are alike, I received then as loneliness. Each new nuance of our experience as parents felt like a separation from those closest to me.

It wasn't until I adored that I realized this empty-lonely wasn't unique to my experience but instead is pervasive across humanity, and that there is only one lasting answer to that loneliness.

I brought the loneliness to His Word.

Loneliness created a thirst in me. Seeing the uniqueness of our children's stories, wanting to have others with which to identify in a stage that seemed primed to bring soul sisters together, left me thirsty. Even in settings with other adoptive moms or mothers of larger families, the nuances of each of our stories with our children—when we brought them home, their sibling dynamics, the way they handled all of the personalities—left me feeling unquenched.

John 4:14 helped me to call what had been loneliness, thirst.

God, what You give me will ensure I never thirst again, I said to Him with my words, though I was unconvinced.

As I gave my mouth and my ache over to His Word, I wore skepticism. Thirst was the predominant feeling, no longer loneliness. The thirst for a witness, someone to know and befriend me in my unique struggles, someone to receive all of me.

Your water springs up into everlasting life, I said His Word back to Him again, feeling as if I were reciting the words of an eighteenth-century poet—words beautiful, majestic, otherworldly, historical, and too distant to be mine.

I brought my skepticism to Him, but He is unwavering in the face of our skepticism.

I pictured the scene in my head. The woman from John 4 to whom He was speaking. (Pause to read John 4:1–26 if you don't recall this scene.) Her history and my skepticism seemed equally unreligious. Jesus doesn't flinch. He saw her in all of her layers, and He talked to her—listened to her, this harlot, whose story He spoke into that day. Her layers didn't deter Him; they focused Him on why He had come.

All the things that made this stage of parenting different from the ones my friends walked through reached across several seasons of my life as I adored. They were no different from all the things that made me unique in the years when my friends birthed babies and I was barren. They were no different from when my friends had thriving newlywed marriages, and we were spending hours in a counselor's office. And on and on.

He doesn't look away. He gives a drink to the lonely.

Picturing His face, the piercing but gentle, knowing eyes of the God-man sitting with this outcast, made me feel my parched mouth and soul and ask for that drink.

Adoring Him as the one who offers living water made me realize how dry my insides were. They made me reach for that water and ask Him to pour His offering into the corridors of my soul, just as He offered to her.

Jesus became real to me as a person — God's personhood — through my adoration.

Though my thirst was not slaked forever after that adoration (isn't that the kind of elusive encounter with God we all want — the one that forever keeps us from weakness?), I knew who to sit with when I felt thirst. I discovered my thirst.

Adoration led me to the well, the one to which I returned. Again and again.

AND HERE, IN THE MIDDLE MINUTES, WE ADORE
FROM JOHN 4:14

You reach the deep. You created the deep parts of me when no eye saw me and You reach those deep parts in the lifetime I live after those first days.

My deep questions do not threaten You — the skepticism, the irreligiosity of my insides when they feel afraid and alone. You reach in. You lean in. You engage.

You are a person, and You respond with your majestic omniscience to me. You see my humanity, and You come close.

You feel me. You know me. You come into the deepest places in me and You revive me. I adore You for reaching my deep. You enter my deep with Your deep, and You heal me, and I come alive.

I adore You, God who created my deep and daily reaches into it.

GOD WHO REACHES DEEP

Psalm 38:9 | Psalm 42:7 | Psalm 51:6 | Psalm 56:8 | Psalm 63:1 | Psalm 107:9 | Psalm 139:1–4 | Psalm 145:16–19 | Isaiah 58:11 | John 4:14 (context: John 4:1–26) | Romans 8:27 | Ephesians 3:14–16

TINY (BIG) PRAYERS

"Lord, all my desire is before You" (Ps. 38:9).
"Deep calls unto deep" (Ps. 42:7).
"My soul thirsts for You" (Ps. 63:1).
"He satisfies the longing soul" (Ps. 107:9).

DIALOGUE WITH HIM

This characteristic of God, which I've positioned later in the book, is broad. Each one of us experiences a need for Him to reach our insides in a unique way. You or your best friend or your mom or your neighbor may all thirst in a way that incites a different angle of Him and a different response.

I leave this portion of one of these last characteristics open ended. I invite you to participate in a life-giving practice we do, nearly daily, in our home: listening prayer.

In the context of adoration, read through each of the verses listed in the "God Who Reaches Deep" section. For those of you who journal, I suggest writing them all out in one spot so you can see them. Then, quiet yourself to listen to what He might be saying to you about yourself as it relates to these passages. Which ones does He highlight? Which ones draw you to linger? *Father, where should I adore?* Listen with a still heart to hear His nudge. And start there. Note what He reveals as you adore back to Him.

And for those of you who don't notice Him highlighting a verse, He promises that His Word never comes back void. He speaks to us through His Word. Choose one verse to start with and adore. But adore expectantly, that in your choosing He will meet you.

28 | GOD WHO BRINGS JUSTICE

What then shall we say to these things? If God is for us, who can be against us?

—ROMANS 8:31

IN THE GRIT

Mothers aren't the only ones who cradle their children's pain, but motherhood is where I learned to hold the inconsolable.

My babies could be rocked to rest, to sleep. We soothed each one of our biological children—the only children we had in our care in their baby years—in their own way, in our arms. Bo needed movement. I wore creases in our carpet with our wooden rocker as I held him close to me in the night hours of his infant days. Virginia craved the nearness of my skin; pressing her face against the nape of my neck brought calm to her tiny body.

Our big kids came to us after the swaddling years. We made up for lost time and held lanky frames in our laps, but some stories aren't soothed in a night. The older they get, the more the injustice of their losses becomes evident. They sit over dinner with a friend who shares her most recent struggle—how a blemish impacts her sense of identity—and they writhe on the inside.

So does their mama.

One morning I wept considering the stories of one of our children. The injustice of loss for a child still with her baby teeth flooded me with anger. The pain she shared with me the night before I now cradled as her mom.

I stumbled upon Romans 8:31. I can't remember how, whether it was the assigned adoration for that day or part of my morning's reading. I believe He ordained it.

I prayed through Romans 8:31 with resistance, and His Spirit reached my hardened insides.

"God is for us," I said without feeling. "God is for me," still hardened. "God is for my kids," and the tears came. The stories of His fight on their behalf flashed through my mind, the reminder of testimonies, mingled with His Word, reviving me.

I adored what I didn't feel and what I questioned, not holding back with my anger and my sadness, and He came.

He reminded me of what was outside of me: Himself, His Word. His Spirit penetrated the unbending walls around my heart, the mama walls that come with cradling the inconsolable, and whispered this word: *God is for us* (Rom. 8:31).

I didn't coach myself that morning. His Spirit led me into truth in the way that only a warm, healing hand applied to the ache can do. The truth: *If God is for us, who can be against us?* (Rom. 8:31).

I circle this mountain often, taking on the hurt of our children as they voice their pain. I need to know, for myself again and again, that the truth of His Word tells the real story better than the circumstances reveal.

Adoration gives me the framework for His narrative in my life and in our children's lives.

AND HERE, IN THE MIDDLE MINUTES, WE ADORE

FROM ROMANS 8:31

You are the God who brings justice.

Your justice isn't theoretical. It has teeth.
Throughout history, You remain just. You live justice
in Your person, God, and You activate that justice
on my behalf.

When I fall victim, You defend. You carry. You
resolve. I can rest in Your justice. It is not my job to
bring justice. You work on my behalf.

I adore You for working on my behalf. As I sleep
and live my day, You act justly. As I field the wrongs
around me, You act justly. You are the final word for
me, God. Your being for me settles it all.

My flesh can rest in hope, O God who brings justice.

I adore You, God of my justice.

GOD WHO BRINGS JUSTICE

Deuteronomy 10:17–18 | Deuteronomy 32:4 | Psalm 33:5 | Psalm 37:28 | Psalm 68:5–6 | Psalm 69:33 | Psalm 89:14 | Psalm 103:6 | Psalm 140:12 | Psalm 146:7 | Isaiah 9:7 | Isaiah 16:5 | Isaiah 42:1–4 | Isaiah 61:1–2 | Jeremiah 9:24 | Luke 18:7–8 | Romans 8:31 | Revelation 21:4–5

TINY (BIG) PRAYERS

"For all His ways are justice" (Deut. 32:4).

"The LORD executes righteousness and justice for all" (Ps. 103:6).

"He will bring forth justice" (Isa. 42:1, 3).

"Shall God not avenge His own elect?" (Luke 18:7).

DIALOGUE WITH HIM

Before we brought home our children, I rarely thought about justice as it relates to God's character and His nature — perhaps because it wasn't personal yet.

Those who seek justice and those who overlook it (I have been both) share something in common: we all need an understanding of God as the one who administers justice.

Using this day's adoration characteristic of God — He brings justice — let's open ourselves up to God's discernment of us. In a few minutes of quiet and solitude, ask Him to reveal to Your heart: *Have I taken on justice as my cause in ways that are independent of You?* or *Have I neglected this side of You, not seeing the need to know You as just?*

With these many characteristics of God behind you in adoration, dip your toes in the water of the intimate and open dialogue with Him that comes through the safety shroud of adoration. Ask Him to reveal your heart to you, and then consider each verse in the "God Who Brings Justice" section and select one or two. Spend time adoring Him through that verse according to what He shows you about your heart.

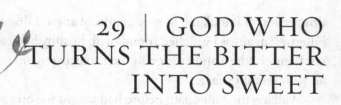

29 | GOD WHO TURNS THE BITTER INTO SWEET

In the light of the king's face is life,
and his favor is like a cloud of the
latter rain.

—PROVERBS 16:15

IN THE GRIT

The darkness from my sister's cancer diagnosis inched closer when I read my own lab reports late one evening. Mystery and suspicion and uncertainty collided for only a few minutes before Google confirmed my fears.

These lab reports marked the beginning of six months of "watch and wait" for one more test that might lead to a slew of others determining my course. Six months of "watch and wait" introduced a brooding cloud over my days. *Can I watch and wait and celebrate the new words of a babe without fearing I might not see her wedding day? Can I watch and wait and be presently joyful when the near future might be dramatically different?*

I knew waiting. Waiting in my infertility, waiting through my dad's cancer, waiting for my marriage to heal. This path of pain and uncertainty was not unfamiliar, but this version of it took me to new depths of angst. I drank the bitterness again as I watched friends with healthy bodies parent their children and engage in their marriages and travel, all with seeming ease.

Walking the bitter path before had taught me one truth: He turns the bitter into sweet.

But telling myself the truths I'd discovered a decade ago fell short. This potential diagnosis had more depth, more implications. I needed to learn His truths again.

One day while reading, I came to Proverbs 16:15, and He flooded my mind. It reads, "In the light of the king's face is life, and his favor is like a cloud of the latter rain."

I knew those clouds. They surfaced, reminding me of the potential diagnosis, as Nate grabbed me around the waist and kissed me in the kitchen. They shrouded the squeals of my littlest ones dumping buckets of water on one another in the pool and when they snuggled in my arms wearing footed pajamas after a bath. The clouds loomed as I talked to my teenage daughters about dating and future husbands.

I could not equate this with favor as Proverbs 16:15 suggests. No way.

I adored Him as I questioned Him, yes, even through Proverbs, which felt like the least heart-informing book of the Bible. Adoration was like smelling salts to my memory, reviving my insides. As if to say the light of my life isn't health, nor is it the security of forever health or long life. It's Him. He is the light of my life.

I adored, and I remembered the God who met me when my youthful body couldn't carry a baby.

I adored, and I felt His presence all over again the way it surrounded me after my dad's cancer diagnosis.

I adored, and I remembered that He met the gaps inside of me when my marriage didn't.

I remembered in story and in science that the clouds—His favor—bring the sweet spring rain. The warm rain shower that produces mist on the ground as it hits the newly sun-bathed pavement. The rain births buds hours after its downpour. The rain waters the thirsty sprigs of spring.

What I defined as threatening (the clouds) was His promise of favor. This was absorbed through my mind, reaching my heart, as I adored.

Adoration became my needed pause. It allowed the memory of His testimonies. It slowed my racing mind. It centered me on His Word, my only sense of security. It brought His presence to the page over time.

Many months of adoration formed an expectancy in me that said, *God will move. He will transform my bitter into sweet.* This expectancy didn't rest on results. As I drove, six months later, to determine the aftermath of "watch and wait," I wept with gratitude as I gripped the steering wheel. The clouds in front of my windshield hung low and brooding, yet I felt grateful for how He met me in my bitter, and felt thankful for how the clouds brought the cleansing spring rain to my petrified insides during all of those months.

At the end of my "watch and wait," I arrived at my fateful appointment, still under the ominous clouds, to hear, "There's nothing there, ma'am."

"This scan is clear," the ultrasound technician said. "I can't find what they identified in June."

Her words, marking the victorious end of my watch-and-wait stretch, were not as significant as His Words over me and through me during that long wait.

You turn the bitter into sweet. Not one bitter moment is exempt from Your leadership. You take every pain, every ache, every loss and turn it into something of Your making.

I adore You, God who infuses every loss and every potential loss with Yourself. You restore with Yourself. You heal with Yourself. You put what was broken back together with Yourself.

You bring clouds that open to release rain. You see the end from the beginning and steward the end from the beginning in my life. At every juncture, You produce the spring rain of Yourself, washing my perspective, healing my insides with the showers of heavy rain.

I adore You, God who turns bitter into sweet.

You take the pain and You lead me to You. I find the You I have desired most in the bitter. I adore You for Your surprise reveal.

GOD WHO TURNS THE BITTER INTO SWEET

Genesis 50:20 | Psalm 30:11 | Psalm 34:17–18 | Psalm 51:8 | Psalm 71:20 | Psalm 147:3 | Psalm 118:5 | Psalm 126 | Proverbs 27:7 | Proverbs 16:15 | Isaiah 35:1–2 | Isaiah 61:1–7 | Romans 2:4 | Romans 5:3–5 | Colossians 1:13 | Ephesians 2:4–5

TINY (BIG) PRAYERS

"The righteous cry out, and the LORD hears" (Ps. 34:17).
"Give them beauty for ashes" (Isa. 61:3).

DIALOGUE WITH HIM

List three or four bitter moments of your life. Sit in each one for a few minutes as you look at your list. I realize that asking this may highlight that these still feel bitter. Plain bitter. (We humans get skilled at pushing through and attempting to press delete on something that isn't finished.)

I encourage you to use this characteristic of God—turning bitter into sweet—to enter into a conversation with Him about those places of bitter pain that still feel unresolved, untouched by Him. This may take some time. (For me, in some bitter areas, it has taken months into years to receive His whispers in these areas.)

We resist because we don't know He can meet us in bitter places. Except, He can. He wants to meet you there.

Adore Him as you consider these bitter spots and ask Him to make something sweet on the inside of you. (Note: adoration requires you to bring all of you. For this characteristic, I encourage you to keep yourself from skipping steps, from answering your pain with the "right" answers. The true healing from pain requires time and tending, not answers.) For some of you, He may shift your circumstances, but often the most significant and most undetected healing happens on the inside. Ask Him, as you adore, to heal your bitter insides. Settle into some months of adoring this side of Him, regularly, as you consider your bitter places.

30 | GOD OF HOPE

For we were saved in this hope, but
hope that is seen is not hope; for
why does one still hope for what he
sees? But if we hope for what we do
not see, we eagerly wait for it with
perseverance.

—ROMANS 8:24–25

IN THE GRIT

Hope is a word I love, and a word I hate.

I carried Hallmark hope in my twenties, the years after I began following God. Better stated: I had fiery eyes for dreaming. Movie scenes flashed through my head as I considered married life. I never admitted that when I twisted my ring around my finger, feeling the sting of our covenant and the reality of our vows, the stark contrast between what I envisioned and what we were living lanced my insides.

Then the years of celebrating and watching friends' families expand while we waited poked holes in my ideals for family. What I once thought was hope was not floating. It couldn't weather delay. It wasn't buoyant.

Bit by bit I learned that my hope wasn't hope at all. I

didn't know hope. I knew a version of idealism and dreaming that was flippant in the circumstantial winds.

This realization set the stage for my first encounter with the God of hope. First He had to dismantle my idealism.

The precursor to my opened womb, thirteen years into marriage, was that I encountered the God of hope. He infused me with that for which I couldn't dream when I had no hope.

But just as He so often does with us, He showed me Himself in layers, revealing about as much as I could handle each time. He had more for me to learn related to hope.

When one of my daughters turned thirteen, I felt ready to deploy the vision I held for this transitional year of her life.

This year will not go untended to, I decided. I made lists and asked questions of friends and sage moms. I planned her year—our year.

It came during an unexpected pregnancy and birth of a child, and smack dab in the middle of navigating a learning disability of another child, while a third child hit a different kind of transitional year that required much attention. And my thirteen-year-old fielded grief anew in such a way that proceeding with my vision for her year, given where she was, seemed inattentive.

My plans were foiled months into the thirteenth year of her life.

Initially, I labeled it as a loss of hope. I'd had hope that in the midst of all the pain of her history, she could experience some normalcy. I'd had hope that we'd hit some life stage "on time." But this was Hallmark hope.

His hope resurrects. When there is little potential for a

future, His hope thrives. I couldn't see it until my hopeful plans for this child died.

Aware of my Hallmark hope, I adored Him for saving me into a hope that doesn't require even a thread of perspective. It doesn't need a thread of dreaming or planning or vision. I could start with nothing and receive His hope. His hope thrives best when I start with nothing. I adored Him through Romans 8:24–25 and other verses and saw that ground zero is the prime place for God to birth a right perspective of His hope.

AND HERE, IN THE MIDDLE MINUTES, WE ADORE

FROM ROMANS 8:24–25

You are the God of hope. To adore You as such requires me to dismantle all that isn't hope. Wistful dreaming, planning under human constraint, circumstantial clinging in the name of prayer and hope—they are not You.

You are hope when I have nothing. You are fuel to a fire that has no embers. You are substance when I bring loss and uncertainty and a lack of eyesight. You birth something out of nothing, God of hope.

When I have a mere taste of You—Your power, Your beauty, Your intent to reach in and save and heal my insides—I wait for nothing but You alone. I do not need to convince myself that You are all I need after I have one brush with You, God of hope, and my heart is revived.

I adore You, God who is retraining my hope and my

eyesight and granting me Your vision when I have
none. In You, I find them.

GOD OF HOPE

Psalm 16:9 | Psalm 31:24 | Psalm 38:15 | Psalm 39:7 | Psalm 42:11 | Psalm 119:114 | Psalm 130:5–7 | Isaiah 40:31 | Lamentations 3:24–27 | John 16:33 | Romans 5:2–5 | Romans 8:23–25 | Romans 15:13 | Ephesians 1:18 | Colossians 1:27 | 1 Peter 1:3–5 | 1 John 3:2–3

TINY (BIG) PRAYERS

"My hope is in You" (Ps. 39:7).
"Hope in the LORD; for with the LORD there is mercy, and with Him is abundant redemption" (Ps. 130:7).
"Now hope does not disappoint, because the love of God has been poured out in our hearts" (Rom. 5:5).
"May the God of hope fill you with all joy and peace in believing" (Rom. 15:13).

DIALOGUE WITH HIM

Because this is our last characteristic of God to pursue within these pages, I encourage you to pause and consider the characteristics in the previous pages that have caught wind in your life as you have adored. Write them out or note them, and then thank God for what He has given you—a greater understanding of Him and of you.

Now from that place of thankfulness, consider an area of hopelessness. For some, this is obvious. For others, like me more recently, it may be the place where your ideals are sky-high and yet not fulfilled. (Hopelessness often gets masked behind idealism.) Take that place to Him and ask

Him to revive your hope as you adore. Select several verses to commit to adoring Him through as this place of hopelessness comes to mind, and watch as He etches out a new definition of hope.

Prepare your heart to receive the radical transformation that hope in God brings to our internal lives.

A Commencement Letter

As you finish these thirty days—or thirty weeks or months—I pray that you finish with anticipation. I think back to my earliest days of practicing adoration without the understanding that this might alter my life. Had I known that then, I might have angled toward life alteration and away from the power of adoration, meeting God in one single moment. I don't want to encourage you to skip steps. I do, however, want to be a whisper of encouragement in your ear. Though not a sage, I hold the experience of hundreds of minutes of conversation with God in the excruciating and in the boring. If I could sit with the twenty-eight- or thirty-year-old me, trying adoration and wondering what's next, the following letter is what I might say. Let it be a commencement letter to you, whether you are twenty-eight or sixty-eight. These words are also for me now, from the forty-two-year-old me to the twenty-eight-year-old me.

> You did it. You identified the gap—the hole in your exchange with God. You resisted ignoring it and instead leaned into it. You chose a rare, rock-ridden path, and you stayed.
>
> The world teaches us to be our harshest critics in an effort to achieve a better mode of living,

a more determined existence. God invites us to another way. Paul said, "I will boast all the more gladly about my weaknesses" (2 Cor. 12:9 NIV). And so do you. You chose a path that exposed the flaws, the foibles, the ways of thinking and being that weren't as neat and tidy as your once thirty-minute quiet times. You diverged from the path the world invited you to tread, and you talked to Him through the rockiness of your everyday life.

Well done.

We resist hearing this, resist receiving it, and resist believing it. But God rejoices over us with gladness, with singing (Zeph. 3:17). He who made us enjoys when we lean, weak, into His voice. When we choose His words over ours, while not dismissing our words as childish or to be ignored, we see His smile lines.

To you, Sara, I give the words that your husband learned to say to you over a decade: "There's no better time to adore, than now, babe." This isn't a once-and-done habit, this engagement with His Word. It will travel with you to weddings and funerals, births and bedsides. In your darkest night and when the sun shines so bright on your face you cannot see its radiance, adoration is your point of access. And adoration is His prize.

When the phone call delivers news. When the child is sick and vomiting for the third night in a row. When the marriage vows are challenged.

When the job isn't what you thought it would be.

I say to you what Nate learned to say: "It's time to adore."

You will never grow tired of telling God who He is and reminding yourself in the process, and finding your weak heart strengthened.

Today, I commission you to ask Him for the strength to adore Him over a lifetime. Instead of highlighting your Bible to prove with pride the verses you have read, see this book as pages ready to be marked and underlined and tear stained by the story of you and God. Of God and you.

Be aware that both your wilderness and your mountaintop will include this kind of conversation with Him. No minute needs to be lived without His tender whispers.

And finally, anticipate the change in your soul. In a year or in five years, ask your spouse, your dearest friends, your family, and especially Him, *How have you seen me grow?* We are our strictest judges. God's kind eyes are often first seen through a close observer. Don't be afraid to note your growth. It will fuel more reaching when no one is looking.

With anticipation,
Sara

ACKNOWLEDGMENTS

Charlotte Mason said, "We who know how little there is in us that we have not received, that the most we can do is to give an original twist, a new application, to an idea that has been passed on to us; [we] recognize, humbly enough, that we are but torch-bearers, passing on our light to the next as we have received it from the last."

Adore is my little torch, with light passed along from so many before me.

Michelle Seidler, thank you for that fateful conversation, the passing of the torch.

And for so many others (more than I can mention) who passed and held and continue to keep the torch as this book releases: thank you.

Mike Salisbury and the Yates and Yates team: my experience with you for the past seven years has proven that you are the best in the field. I love my team.

Alicia Kasen, Stephanie Smith, Trinity McFadden, Brian Phipps, and the others at Zondervan: thank you for not only stewarding this work but enhancing it by what you do. It is a joy to work with this family of people.

Lauren Chandler: your words here are a great gift.

And to my research team—Hannah Robinson, Cherish Smith, Annie Kawase, Rachael Steele, Erica Nork, Mary Arntsen, and Telma Weisman: thank you for the hidden hours you poured into forming these pages.

To my prayer team: you all are the secret strength behind this book and my ministry. I am so grateful for how you sow in secret.

Mandie Joy Turner: you gave this idea creative wings long before I had a vision for it. And Erica Nork: your behind-the-scenes collision of heart and skill is a profound gift to my ministry. My friendships with you both as we work make my writing life rich.

And to my friends who know the intricacies of this writing and mothering life of mine: your prayers, words of encouragement, and friendship have upheld me.

Lily, Hope, Eden, Caleb, Bo, Virginia, and Charlotte: you already carry the light He gave me to pass to you. Each one of you makes my world so much better.

Nate: some days, I wonder if this book writing is merely an excuse to partner with my favorite person on the earth and do great exploits together.

And finally, You, God. You passed me the message so many have carried before me, all so that I could find You more in the carrying of it. I'll say yes again if only it means more of You.

NOTES

1. A. W. Tozer, *The Knowledge of the Holy* (New York: Harper and Brothers, 1961), 10.
2. Tim Keller, "Prayers That Don't Work," *Desiring God*, October 13, 2014, https://www.desiringgod.org/interviews/prayers-that-dont-work.
3. Laura Hackett Park, "You Satisfy My Soul," *You Satisfy My Soul*, Forerunner Music, 2013.
4. C. S. Lewis, *Reflections on the Psalms* (New York: Harcourt, Brace and Company, 1958), 93.
5. Brent Curtis and John Eldredge, *Sacred Romance* (Nashville: Thomas Nelson, 1997), 164.
6. Eugene H. Peterson, *Traveling Light: Modern Meditations on St. Paul's Letter of Freedom* (Colorado Springs: Helmers and Howard, 1998), 83.
7. C. S. Lewis, *Letters to Malcolm: Chiefly on Prayer* (New York: Harper Collins, 1992), 122.
8. Tim Keller, *Prayer: Experiencing Awe and Intimacy with God* (New York: Penguin Group, 2014), 190.
9. John Calvin, *Institutes of the Christian Religion*, 1536 edition, trans. Ford Lewis Battles (Grand Rapids: Eerdmans, 1995), 15.

10. Raymond Ortlund Jr., *Proverbs: Wisdom That Works* (Wheaton, IL: Crossway, 2012), 32.

11. Henri Nouwen, *Here and Now: Living in the Spirit* (New York: Crossroad, 1994), 88.

12. Douglas Steere, *Prayer and Worship* (New York: Edward W. Hazen Foundation, distributed by Association Press, 1938), 34, quoted in Richard Foster, *Prayer: Finding the Heart's True Home* (New York: Harper Collins, 1992), 145.

13. Dallas Willard, *Renovation of the Heart* (Colorado Springs: NavPress, 2002), 95.

14. Curt Thompson, *The Soul of Shame* (Downers Grove, IL: InterVarsity Press, 2015), 178.

15. John Piper, *Desiring God* (Sisters, OR: Multnomah, 1986), 137.

16. A. W. Tozer, *Essays on Prayer* (Downers Grove, IL: InterVarsity Press, 1968), 2.

17. Tozer, *Essays on Prayer*, 3.

18. Richard Foster, *Prayer: Finding the Heart's True Home* (New York: Harper Collins, 1992), 145.

19. Foster, *Prayer*, 153.

20. Lewis, *Letters to Malcolm*, 119.

21. Brother Lawrence quoted in Tozer, *Essays on Prayer*, 6.

22. Foster, *Prayer*, 157.

23. Thompson, *Soul of Shame*, 99.

24. Charles Spurgeon, "Imitators of God," Sermon #1725, Metropolitan Tabernacle, Newington, June 10, 1883.

Every Bitter Thing Is Sweet

Tasting the Goodness of God in All Things

Sara Hagerty

Sara Hagerty found Him when life stopped working for her. She found Him when she was a young adult mired in spiritual busyness and when she was a newlywed bride with doubts about whether her fledgling marriage would survive. She found Him alone in the night as she cradled her longing for babies who did not come. She found Him as she kissed the faces of children on another continent who had lived years without a mommy's touch.

In *Every Bitter Thing Is Sweet*, Hagerty weaves fabric from the narrative of her life into the mosaic of a Creator who mends broken stories. Here you will see a God who is present in every changing circumstance. Most significant, you see a God who is present in every unchanging circumstance as well.

Whatever lost expectations you are facing—in family, career, singleness, or marriage—*Every Bitter Thing Is Sweet* will bring you closer to a God who longs for you to know Him more.

Going beyond the narrative to offer timeless insight, Hagerty brings you back to hope, back to healing, back to a place that God is holding for you alone, a place where the unseen is more real than what the eye can perceive. A place where every bitter thing is sweet.

Available in stores and online!

Unseen

The Gift of Being Hidden in a World That Loves to Be Noticed

Sara Hagerty

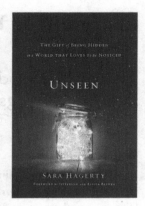

Every heart longs to be seen and understood. Yet most of our lives is unwitnessed. We spend our days working, driving, parenting. We sometimes spend whole seasons feeling unnoticed and unappreciated. So how do we find contentment when we feel so hidden?

In *Unseen*, Sara Hagerty suggests that this is exactly what God intended. He is the only one who truly knows us. He is the only one who understands the value of the unseen in our lives. When this truth seeps into our souls, we realize that only when we hide ourselves in God can we give ourselves to others in true freedom and know the joy of a deeper relationship with the God who sees us.

Through an eloquent exploration of both personal and biblical story, Hagerty calls us to offer every unseen minute of our lives to God. God is in the secret places of our lives that no one else witnesses. But we've not been relegated to these places. We've been invited.

We may be "wasting" ourselves in a hidden corner today: The cubicle on the fourth floor. The hospital bedside of an elderly parent. The laundry room. But these are the places God uses to meet us with a radical love. These are the places that produce the kind of unhinged love in us that gives everything at His feet, whether or not anyone else ever proclaims our name, whether or not anyone else ever sees.

God's invitation is not just for a season or a day. It is the question of our lives: "When no one else applauds you, when it makes no sense, when you see no results will you waste your love on Me?"

Available in stores and online!